Teach Me How To Love

A True Story That Touches Hearts And Helps With The Laundry!

Scott Kalechstein Grace

ISBN: 061549210X
ISBN-13: 9780615492100

Writing a book is not a solo affair...

Great gobs of gratitude to the following people for their valuable encouragement, constructive criticism, and helpful editing suggestions: Venus Elyse, Chia Longtree, Paul Ferrini, Joyce and Ken Dvoren, David Presler, Aspen Green, Rev. Carolyn Carter, Shepherd Hoodwin, Susan Doty, Trish Turpel, Lee Glickstein, Corinne Smith, Susan Velasquez, Jon Cotton, Rebecca Zimman, Karen Bentley, Barbara Leuin, Karen Lee, Melanie Sears, Elizabeth Severino, Ricki Blanchard, Bobbie Woods, Lygia, Beverly Brunelle, Matt Regan, Ayleyaell, Sheryl Valentine, Margy Michael, Cary Seibel, Alfred Stulginskas, and Shirley Norwood.

Special thanks to Aspen Green for her selfless service to this project, her time, skill, generosity, and positive energy, and to Mia Alexander (http://miaalexander.artistwebsites.com) for her artistry with the back photo, and her love-filled Caribbean cooking.

Praise For
Teach Me How To Love

"Teach Me How To Love grips and grabs you like a thriller, except that instead of scaring you, it will encourage you to laugh your fears away. Scott manages to be honest, entertaining, inspirational, and wildly funny throughout-and even when the tale turns profound and deeply healing, somehow it all still goes down light and easy, with humor as a constant companion. This is my kind of book!"

-Gary Renard, author of *The Disappearance of The Universe*

"I have watched Scott grow and know he is real. *Teach Me How to Love* is full of love, laughter and tears, the necessary ingredients for a story that will touch your heart, and yes, help with the laundry!"

-Dr. Bernie Siegel, author of *Love, Medicine and Miracles*

"Teach Me How To Love delights and disarms with humor, and then takes you by surprise with its transformational teachings. Scott Grace generously points the way to courageous living and loving, all while keeping it fresh, delightful, and so very fun. If you have a sneaking suspicion that you can use more lightening up as you reach for your dreams, then read this book!"

-Jack Canfield, author of *The Success Principles* and co-author of *Chicken Soup for the Soul*

"*Teach Me How To Love* is a captivating, illuminating and joyously entertaining guidebook for our soul. As you laugh and cry your way through the pages, you will come to recognize yourself. I thank Scott for his unique gifts and courage to share them. They will shine light upon your own."

-Alan Cohen, author of *A Daily Dose of Sanity* and *The Dragon Doesn't Live Here Anymore*

"Scott Grace's joy is contagious and lights up every page of this entertaining and inspiring book. This is a brilliant account of happiness that comes from the inside out. His remarkable story of going from laundry bag street peddler to transformational troubadour will loosen your cares, fuel your enthusiasm, and help remind you of your own infinite capacity to love and be loved."

-Marci Shimoff, author of *Love for No Reason*, Co-Author of *Chicken Soup for The Woman's Soul*

"Imagine a motivational and inspirational speaker/comedian/singer with a generous heart, twinkling wit, and disarming honesty, and you have a glimpse of Scott Grace. *Teach Me How To Love* sparkles with fun, wisdom and great humor as Scott relates the ins and outs, from very personal experience, of daring to live intentionally. It also happens to be the finest kind of love story, one that not only gives you hope and goose bumps, but also tools and a treasure map to your heart. You may just enjoy reading it so much that you don't even realize how much you're being healed!"

-Tama J. Kieves, author of *THIS TIME I DANCE! Creating the Work You Love*

"The world lives to hear love stories, and Scott's is a doosey! *Teach Me How To Love* is a story that will help so many people who are on the fence, afraid to commit (and who isn't!), and to move into the greatness of love."

-Shannon and Scott Peck, co-authors of *The Love You Deserve*

"*Teach Me How To Love* is utterly brilliant. The writing is genius. I love the blend of extraordinary humor with the insightful wrap on the simple, the mundane and the deep stuff of life – all mixed together like a big club sandwich oozing with layers of fulfilling filling. It's meaty, it's fun, and it resonates deeply."

-Susie Pearl, author of *Master Mind*

"*Teach Me How to Love* is a wonderful, authentic story of personal awakening. Scott's journey from selling laundry bags on the streets of New York to becoming a singer, songwriter and minister of love is inspiring and wise. It will touch your heart."

-Paul Ferrini, author of *Love Without Conditions* and *The Silence of the Heart*

"*Teach Me How to Love* offers the reader an exceptional opportunity to be uplifted, inspired, awakened and entertained by storytelling at its finest. Scott has mastered the alchemy of turning life experience into lessons in levity. Read it, breathe with it, smile with it, and share it with a friend!"

-Donald Epstein DC, author of *The Twelve Stages Of Healing*

"*Teach Me How To Love* is all about love. Scott Grace manages to unfold his own love story with such warmth, humor, honesty, and wit, you will find yourself irresistibly drawn in, cheering, crying, laughing, and learning as you go."

–Barry & Joyce Vissell, authors of
The Shared Heart and *Meant To Be*

"*Teach Me How To Love* somehow sneaks in the secrets to lasting love and healthy relationships while keeping you enthralled, laughing, and on the edge of your seat throughout. Bravo to Scott Grace for combining profound wisdom and escapist entertainment all in one wonderful book!"

- Jon Mundy, publisher of *Miracles Magazine* and author of
Living A Course in Miracles

"*Teach Me How To Love* is one from the heart and for the heart. Scott's gift of humor, combined with his eloquent transparency and vulnerability, will take you on a journey to the depths of your own capacity to love. Expect lots of laughter, a few tears, and plenty of precious pearls of wisdom along the way."

-Paul and Layne Cutright, authors of *You're Never Upset for the Reason You Think* and *Straight From the Heart*

"Got ENLIGHTENMENT? Then read this book! Scott Grace exposes his own raw revelations on his own path into intimacy, through the treacherous terrain of the core conflict in relationships between self-connection/Freedom and other connection/Love. *Teach Me How To Love* will tickle your funny bone and lift your spirits as it raises your consciousness."

-Kelly Bryson MFT, Author of *Don't Be Nice, Be Real*

"Scott's lovely, lively story flows from laughter to tears and back exactly the way a juicy life asks of us when we tune into the musical comedy of the soul. Don't let *Teach Me How To Love* pass you by!"

-Lee Glickstein, author of *Be Heard Now*

Table of Contents

Part One.... Following My Heart

Part Two....Opening My Heart

Foreword

By Alan Cohen

I have known Scott Grace since 1984, and I have always respected him. Even at a young age Scott shined with rare inspiration, clarity, and willingness to be real. If there was ever an old soul in a young body, it was Scott.

When I first met Scott he was making his living hawking laundry bags on the streets of New York City. (There, I thought, is a powerful education!). Scott boldly positioned himself on busy street corners and (in between dodging police) sang rap songs about his laundry bags. I am certain that a fair amount of customers contributed to Scott's cause not so much because they needed a bag, but because they wanted to reward him for the entertainment and creativity he exuded.

Then Scott went on to become a full-time musician and speaker. Again he displayed an unusual talent in manufacturing clever songs in the moment. He would stand before a person or a group and channel music and lyrics perfectly appropriate to the listeners. Free now to share his gifts without looking over his shoulder for the law, he went even deeper into a unique and personal service.

Scott and I lived together for a while in *A Course in Miracles* study community. It was there that I came to appreciate his honesty. On many occasions Scott showed awesome courage to share what he felt, even at the risk of embarrassment or possible rejection. And in each case his friends only loved him more for his authenticity.

Now Scott has written a book chronicling his path and his lessons, and it is a wonderful one. *Teach Me How To Love* is the story of one humble yet powerful man carving out his path in life, trusting his heart as his guide. What more could any of us do? Surely the lessons of life are not hidden in some distant heaven, forcing us to climb to the top of the Himalayas to find the truth. No, everything we need to know and learn is right before us, right where we are. We always magnetize the perfect people and experiences to take our next step. As you read Scott's story and insights, you will be inspired to extract the gold of life from the mine upon which you are standing.

I would like to call your attention to Scott's story of a healing he affected in his relationship with his mother. It started when Scott took a risk and invited his mother to a five-day retreat intended to deepen the bonds between parents and their children. Although Scott fully expected his mom to say no, she accepted, and the unfolding story of their healing is magnificent and moving. It is this kind of courage we all need if we are going to find the kind of peace we seek. We must reach out beyond our comfort zone to make contact with those from whom we feel separate. This is the real spiritual work before us, and as we come to trust love more than fear, we will enjoy the rewards we long for.

Teach Me How To Love is a captivating, illuminating, and joyously entertaining guidebook for our soul. As you laugh and cry your way through the pages, you will come to recognize yourself.

I thank Scott for his unique gifts and courage to share them. They will shine light upon your own.

Author's Introduction

Passing The Torch

One winter's day in 1987, while I was waiting to use the restroom at a McDonald's, an elderly woman in a wheelchair came in, and her caregiver asked me if they could go ahead of me. "Of course!" I told her. As she was escorted into the bathroom, I noticed a beautiful glow in her eyes, which reminded me of the eyes of a baby: bright blue, crystal clear, pure and precious.

Two minutes passed slowly, and finally I heard the sweet sound of a toilet flushing. Both women came out smiling, and before I knew what was happening, the older one wheeled herself right up to me, slowly rose out of her wheelchair, kissed me on the lips and said, "Thank you. I love you." She came into my arms and offered her frail body in a delicate and tender embrace. Her eyes blazed with life and love, and I felt a warm ripple spread throughout my chest. She sat back down and was escorted out. I also took a seat, to collect myself and to reflect on what had just happened. The woman's eyes, her radiant spirit, and especially her innocent and courageous offering of love had me shaking. I was in delicious shock, thrown completely into a state of wonder. It seems life's best moments catch us off guard, sneaking up on us when we least expect it, and this was surely one of them.

My mind, that endless question machine, was spinning. Who was that woman? Was she too old and senile to remember that one doesn't go around kissing strangers on the lips, or was she too wise to allow her heart to be confined to the ways of the world? My thoughts raced with theories and questions that would never be answered. Finally, I gave up and just let it be. For the rest of the day I could not wipe a smile off my face.

I'm happy to say that I never fully recovered from that experience. It was as if she had passed a torch on to me, igniting my desire to love boldly, to live without concern for what the neighbors might think. The torch burned a hole in my tolerance for mediocre, half-asleep self-expression. I wanted what this woman had, and I didn't want to wait till I was that old before I was that free.

But how would I do it? What was my way of expressing love? Images danced through my mind about what I might say and do. Would I kiss strangers on the lips and tell them I loved them? Pretty soon I realized that I couldn't approach this business of loving with a plan of action. It had to spring up from my heart like a bubbly fountain, spontaneous and unrehearsed. All I could do was practice being a vessel for love, not its controller. From the depths of my being, I asked to learn the ways of love, and my prayer took the form of a song:

Teach Me How To Love

I want to wake up in the morn, and know what I'm made of
Oh, Great Spirit, teach me, teach me how to love
I want to hear the birds at dawn, and know what they sing of

Oh, Great Spirit, teach me, teach me how to love
I've learned quite well just how to hide
Behind these rusty walls inside
But now my heart is calling me to rise above
Teach me how to love

I've shined on just a chosen few that fit me like a glove
Oh, Great Spirit, teach me, teach me how to love
Teach me to shine on everyone just like the sun above
Oh, Great Spirit, teach me, teach me how to love
I've walked the earth in self-defense
Bracing for some punishment
Could it be I'm safer here?
I've asked a jury of my fears
I'd rather ask a dolphin or a dove
Teach me how to love

1987 © ScottSongs

The more I learn about love, the more I feel like a beginner. I am amazed to read that scientists estimate that the average human being uses 5 to 10% of their brain. I suspect that we are all beginners in matters of the heart, too.

When I wrote the song *Teach Me How To Love* I was admitting I knew next to nothing about loving and being loved. I was asking sincerely to be taught. This book covers what I've learned so far.

Part 1 is about learning to follow my heart and trust my intuition, especially in regard to my music and speaking career. It goes down easy, as good humor makes for good digestion. With levity still a constant companion, the second half goes deeper into my experiences of growth and transformation through relationships

I started writing this in 1995, and wrote fifteen chapters that year. What took me so long to finish? I needed to live more of my life and learn more of my love lessons so I could be in integrity with what I was writing about. It was as if the book was far more wise and mature than I was. I needed to catch up with it.

For instance, when Alan Cohen wrote the Foreword in 1996, I was uncomfortable with what he wrote about the healing I supposedly had with my mother. He wrote about it as if it was one of the most moving parts of the book. Yet at that time I had just briefly touched the surface in writing about my mother. More importantly, I had not come close to forgiveness and peace in that relationship. My Mom and I had a long ways to grow. But I took his words as a challenge, a prophetic invitation to go deeper with my Mom. Years later I had a healing with her that indeed felt like a miracle. I was then able to finish the chapter that Alan must have intuitively known was in me to write.

One of my neighbors, Jack Kornfield, wrote a fabulous book called *After the Ecstasy, the Laundry,* about bringing our spiritual peaks into the often-mundane valleys of everyday life. My story starts with the laundry...or, more precisely, with nylon laundry bags and a very odd sales job. In that vocation, which was a far cry from doing what I love, I learned to bring love to what I was doing. I discovered how easy it is to make people's day, and how that can bring the ecstasy and the laundry together. It's where I first practiced passing on the torch that was handed to me years ago in McDonald's by an ageless and liberated woman unafraid of expressing her love.

The torch is now being passed to you in the form of this book. *Teach Me How To Love* is meant to be caught and spread, not just read. It's my wish that you let it ignite the flame of your passion, and that you then play it forward and pass the torch on to others in your own unique way.

If you've been sitting on your assets for a long time, the good news is that it might be hard to take this book sitting down. You might just find that it moves you up and out of whatever chair you've been in, moving you to sing, dance, write, serve, forgive, express love and celebrate life with your whole heart and soul. If you're waiting till you're perfect or even close to it, you might just put it off indefinitely. If you dare to live like you already have (and are) something wonderful to share, life will meet your daring and give you a starring role in a play. Your play.

As one of my songs says, "Life is too short to be a spectator sport!"

I'll see you on the stage. Let the play begin.

PART ONE
Following My Heart

Chapter One

The Odd Job

Why do dolphins leap joyful from the sea? Why do the morning birds sing? Why does the earth dance in trees and reach forests to the sun? Why do children play? This is a recreational universe. When you remember the play that lifted your heart as a child, you will know the heart of God.

-Ken Carey, The Third Millennium

"**N**YLON JUMBO LAUNDRY BAGS! MACHINE WASHABLE! WATER RESISTANT!" Uttered at the top of my vocal volume range, I repeated these words for seven years as I worked the sidewalks of New York City as an unlicensed, self-employed, street peddler. I bought the bags below wholesale, straight from a factory in North Carolina, and made a great profit selling them just below retail. I loved the quick cash and the gutsy, streetwise calluses that formed on my psyche. I was part of the color and pulse of New York, a place where adrenaline, art and survival all blended together in a tapestry of shadows and light.

My style for hawking the laundry bags became something of a creative, comic performance. "How did you get into this?" people asked me as I handed them their purchase. "How do I get out of this?" became the question I asked daily as the call of a career in music grew louder and my patience for eluding the police grew thinner.

Did I say police? Yes, I confess! This crazy job of mine was not exactly legal. "Slightly illegal" was my juicy rationalization. About once a week I got caught, collected a ticket, and had to hand over a sack of laundry bags to the City of New York, via the police. Did breaking the law nag at my conscience? Not at all. Well, at least not my conscious conscience. I was a rebel without a pause, enjoying the game of cops and robbers, and moving too fast to question my ethics or my sanity. Besides, I was also using the job to fine-tune my meditation skills.

My discipline was called Zen and The Art of Spotting the Cops Before They See You. This spiritual practice for finding inner strength in the inner city found me routinely in the Yoga posture of being on my toes, my head stretching from left to right, focused like a laser beam in the here and now. The police sometimes dressed in civilian clothes, immersing themselves amongst the human sardines that swamped the city sidewalks on any given day. I developed a sixth sense, an organically grown synthesis of intuition and paranoia. I could spot the police, pack up my bags, and slip into the crowd at a speed that Houdini would have admired. But even with my escape skills honed to a science, I did get busted on occasion. It was part of the job.

While tempted to let those instances dampen my day, I took it upon myself to make light of the moments when the police were writing me tickets and confiscating my bags. Feather dusting the situation with levity, I refused to buy into the attitude of doom and gloom.

One day an outrageous idea crossed my mind. I have learned to spring into action when a creative prompting knocks on my door. Before hesitation festered into analysis, which almost always leads to paralysis, I took out my pen and wrote:

To The Proud Officers Of The New York City Police Dept,

This note is written permission for my son, Scott, to sell laundry bags on the streets of the city without a license. I know it is against the law, but my son is such a good boy in almost every other aspect of his life. I think he is entitled to some leeway here. This note officially absolves him from the law. Ignorance of the law is no excuse, but a mother's written permission sure is!

Hugs and kisses,
Mom

I put the note in my pocket and waited, almost eagerly, for the next time I was caught in the act, bags in hand. Sure enough, my sales were interrupted the next day by two blue-clad members of the N.Y.P.D. "Hold it!" I confidently barked. "I've got a pardon!" I handed one of the officers my note. He read it out loud in official police business monotone. Neither of them had any change of facial expression, and for a moment I feared the worst. Trying to humor a New York City police officer, committed to the confines of seriousness, can have disastrous results. Finally, the pregnant moment gave birth to a response: "Take a walk! This one's on Mom!" I put my bags over my shoulder and skipped away a free man, thankful for the juices of creativity that turned a potentially negative situation into a close encounter of the hilarious kind.

The next day I was selling in the same location when a police car careened out of nowhere, flashing lights and blasting sirens, and screeched to a halt on the sidewalk, a breath away from my body. The two officers from yesterday were right in my face before I even realized that they were after me. But instead of my bags, it seemed I was in possession of a rare and precious piece of literature. "We want the note!" one of them said, as if expecting me to challenge their authority. I handed him the scribbled piece of evidence. "We told everybody in the precinct about it, but they didn't believe us. We're going to laminate it and post it on the bulletin board!" I relaxed, realizing that the sirens and the flashing lights were part of a joke they were playing to get back at me. So there we were, three human beings, sharing an odd and playful moment, temporarily suspending the crime and punishment game and connecting at a level that the script did not call for.

Perhaps the finest moments of connection happen when we are willing to abandon the popular script and improvise our own.

Sometimes my silly sales tactics included barking things like, "You've Read The Book. You've Seen The Movie! NOW BUY THE BAG!!" Other times I would proclaim with authority, "The Strongest Laundry Bag You Can Buy Without A Prescription!" Some people enjoyed a good laugh as they passed. Others would quicken their pace and be careful not to smile or make eye contact and possibly catch whatever I seemed to have! Maybe on some level they knew that playfulness could be contagious, dangerously spread through inner child-to-child contact, and often renders its victims quite vulnerable to subversive and spontaneous emissions of joy and laughter.

When my laundry bags or my humor were not well received, I got to work on some of my rejection issues. My sidewalk escapades became adventures in personal growth, time and space to slip out of self-consciousness and develop some confidence, as well as some cockiness! I look back on those days with affection, amused and grateful that I actually did it, and even more grateful that I don't do it anymore!

Six months after selling my last laundry bag and moving to California, I went back to New York to visit friends and family. I couldn't resist paying a visit to Court Street in Brooklyn Heights, where many of my bags were sold. I strolled into the Kosher Pizzeria that had become my hangout over the years. The employees gave me a warm greeting. One of the waiters, visibly excited, handed me a copy of the most recent edition of the *Brooklyn Heights Gazette.* On the back page was a comic strip with yours truly in it. An artist had captured me in caricature, selling my wares on Court Street. The caption read, "Whatever happened to the laundry bag man?" I had left my mark on the streets of the city I grew up in! That felt good.

A few years later I was back in Brooklyn to give a concert. A woman in the front row of the audience was looking at me quite strangely all throughout the performance. She appeared dazed, confused and disoriented. At the concert's close she approached me. "I know you from somewhere," she said painfully, as she attempted to make a difficult withdrawal from her memory bank.

I looked into her eyes and instantly knew. "NYLON JUMBO LAUNDRY BAGS!" I exclaimed with a huge smile spread across my face. Her eyes registered both shock and the relief of recognition. "Oh, my God!" she exclaimed. "You were the laundry bag man!" She had cracked the case, but there were more pieces of the puzzle to put together. "I passed you on Court Street for years, feeling so sorry for you. What happened? How did you get off the streets?" She had many more questions, wanting to know the details of how I had created such a rewarding career doing what I love. It was obvious that her belief system did not have much room for the possibility of people transforming their lives for the better, yet there I was, guitar in hand, proof before her eyes. I walked her to her car, telling her more of my story; voice lessons, recording my music, making my "no more bags" commitment, moving to California, taking the leap, trusting the universe. Her reactions gave me a richer appreciation for my bags to riches journey. What a tale to tell around the campfire!

Sometimes remembering those days feels like a sketchy recall of a past life memory. Did I really spend seven years in this life as a street peddler, running from the police like a criminal? Yes, and with no regrets. I made warm, human, and creative contact with each of my customers, sending each of them off with some positive vibes along with their purchase. I made friends with the homeless, and even sang rap songs to the passing high school students. (*I don't mean to boast, I don't mean to brag, but I've got the world's best laundry bags! They're a bargain for you, they're a profit for me. If you buy a couple dozen, I'll give you one for free!*)

What had started as simply a laundry bag sales job, just in it for the money, evolved into a laundry bag performance ministry, where I went to work each day excited and eager to make a small difference in people's lives, to bring a little levity to their gravity. It strikes me sometimes that although I have changed products, in all these years I have not really changed jobs. My job has always been about sharing joy and celebrating life, and that is always the business at hand, whether it is gift wrapped in singing, writing, or selling NYLON JUMBO LAUNDRY BAGS!

A Little Levity

There is a remedy for any ill
It's over the counter and it's not in a pill
When you're all hot and bothered it will get you to chill
With no side effects at all

A little levity when you're not at your best
A little levity when life is hard to digest
It puts the Rolaids to your acid test
So come on now and get some relief

I have some allergies but not to hay
My ego breaks out when things don't go my way
But I need no antihistamine to save the day
My cure is already inside

A little levity saves you cash on your meds
A little levity beats Viagra in bed
It gets a rise out of your sleepy head
And res-erects your life

There's enough heavy stuff weighing down on humanity
May I suggest a lighter consciousness
Losing weight through levity

When telemarketers pay you a call
Don't let them drive you right up the wall
Pretend that it's phone sex and just have a ball
In no time they'll be getting off!

A little levity when you're running amuck
A little levity when your hair day sucks
A little dab of it is more than enough
To smooth out your split ends
A little levity when you're feeling down
A little levity makes your joy abound
Your heart was never meant to touch the ground
So come on now and flap on your wings

A little levity that's how angels fly
A little levity is gonna get you high
Blow all your worries a big kiss goodbye
A little levity makes gravity fun

1993 © ScottSongs

Chapter Two

Finding My Voice

I sing. I've been singing for my supper full time since 1990, and I am happy to say that I have never gone hungry...although people who have observed me chow down after a concert might disagree. I pay bills on time, have not been in debt, and manage to feed my retirement fund most months.

People who hear me sing often assume that I've been at it forever. The truth is that for a good chunk of my life I did not sing, believing I did not have a good enough voice to partake of the festivities.

I was one of those people who believed you are either born with a natural talent for singing or you are doomed to be a non-singer all your life. This was a curious thought, since in childhood I had started from scratch with both the violin and guitar, and stumbled through learning to play them over time. When I took violin lessons I trusted that through practice and diligence I would learn to play the violin. When I took up guitar I was confident that I would eventually, with the help of my weekly lessons and practicing, become an adequate guitar player. Yet somehow it did not register that I could take singing lessons and learn how to sing. Much to my delight I discovered that the voice is just another instrument, and that it can be developed through exercises, practice and persistence, just like any other. In a few years I went from playing my guitar without singing to making my own recordings and putting myself out in the world as a professional singer. What happened? How did I take such a leap? I'm glad you asked....

In my two-year stint as a student at the University of Buffalo I took an anthropology course called Magic, Witchcraft And Sorcery. This was a fascinating study that sent my young mind soaring with ideas to ponder. Basically, under the guise of anthropology, we were learning about the power of beliefs. We learned about how refugees from Haiti had been mysteriously dying in Florida hospitals. Doctors could find nothing wrong with them and were unable to help. Then someone summoned a Haitian witch doctor, who diagnosed the remaining patients as the recipients of a spell. He recited some incantations over the sick people, and color instantly came back to their skin. They walked out of the hospital within hours!

We also learned about a native tribe in Africa that believed that having babies had nothing to do with having sex. These people had no concept of or need for birth control. The women in the tribe would freely have intercourse for years with no pregnancy. One day they would receive a vision of a soul wanting to be born. In an altered state they would experience being impregnated by Spirit. Their experience of conception was completely non-sexual!

The course opened my eyes to the relative nature of reality. At the conclusion, the professor recommended a few books to those of us who were interested in further study. One of those books was *Illusions*, by Richard Bach. *Illusions* became my bible, and I carried it around everywhere. Through that book and others like it, Life was saying to me, "Scott, you can do anything you truly want to do. All limitations are illusions held in place by your worship of the concept, *impossible*. Take that away and the whole game changes."

What does this have to do with singing? Lots! Although I adored music and songwriting, I had successfully convinced myself that I was not and never could be good enough to pursue it as a career. Talk about casting a spell! When I left college music was just a hobby. I had written a few songs, but I didn't sing them in front of others. I had no confidence in my musical talents, although secretly I fantasized about becoming a singer. I was very surprised when one of my trainers at the end of a class I had been taking on learning to lead seminars took me aside and said, "Scott, I'm rarely wrong about these things. When I look into your eyes, I see music. My sense is that music will become a very important part of your life purpose."

Her prophecy was exciting to my heart, and threatening to my ego, which had grown quite fond of playing it small in regards to playing my music. Although I could feel a kettle of songs brewing inside of me, I was convinced that becoming a singer was a fantasy not worth indulging. Keeping a lid on it seemed a lot safer than the vulnerability of admitting my passion. But the stove had been turned on and the teapot was starting to whistle. My secret dream was reaching its boiling point.

One day I was listening to a barbershop quartet singing doo-wop a cappella on a street corner in Greenwich Village. This was a regular pastime for me, and as usual, I was singing along under my breath. I felt enchanted, swept away by the beautiful harmonies. Then one of the singers in the circle asked his buddies, "Hey, does anyone know the lead to that new Billy Joel song on the radio, *The Longest Time?*" Everybody lit up, knowing it was a perfect song for their style of singing, but no one knew the lyrics all the way through. They were about to drop it and start on another song, when a hand went up from somewhere within the audience. I noticed it was attached to my arm. Then a voice piped up, coming somewhere from the vicinity of my throat. "I know the song!" I exclaimed, in a tone of authority

I must have borrowed from the gods. The quartet, slightly surprised that someone outside their circle was inviting himself to lead a song, invited me into the center. My knees were shaking, and I wasn't imitating Elvis. I was so scared I'm convinced my angelic cheerleaders were working overtime to help me get through this. The quartet started the song with the background *oohs*. I opened my mouth and started singing. I noticed some pleasant vibrato in my voice that I had never heard before. Maybe it was from the trembling.

When the song was over, the quartet and the audience applauded me. I slipped away from the crowd and started skipping down the street, aware that I just had a life changing experience, and that I was through hiding and pretending. Music was not just a hobby. It was a passion, and I burned to find out if there was a singing voice in there to discover. I started taking voice lessons, but even more significant than that, I started singing, in front of people, at any opportunity.

I remember a deal I made with God at that time. *"OK, you gave me this love of music and song. I can't think of anything in the world I'd rather do than celebrate life through singing. I'm going to bet that if you planted in me the dream-seed, then you will guide me on the path of having it come to fruition. I'm going to take these lessons. I'm also going to sing, privately and publicly, at any chance I get. I'm going to become a singing fool! And I will trust that with each song I sing, I am being guided to develop a beautiful voice that I can use to spread joy on this planet. God, here's the deal: I'll open my mouth. You make me a singer!!"*

Well, I did follow through on my part of the deal. I sang in my apartment. I sang for my friends. I sang on the sidewalks of

Greenwich Village and in Washington Square Park. I took weekly voice lessons and did my daily exercises, and gradually noticed improvement. With each week, there was a little more space and range of sound in my throat. It was as if I was building a vocal pipeline for the sweetness of my soul to find expression. My friends noticed my progress and told me so. Their support was a valuable part of my confidence building.

I remember when I met Charley Thweatt, who gave me a great gift with his encouragement. Charley travels globally as an inspirational troubadour, and had been doing so for many years when we met. He travels to exotic places in the world and does exactly what I was aspiring to do with music. Charley has a beautiful singing voice, and I was instantly insecure, intimidated, and jealous of his gifts and success. I managed to put those feelings aside long enough to spend some delightful, playful, connecting time with him. We took out our guitars and shared songs. When we finished, Charley looked into my eyes and projected a laser beam of love and support my way. After a minute or two of precious, penetrating eye contact, he broke the silence with words that sailed into my heart like a shooting star. "Scott, I think your music is meant to be heard and appreciated by many, many people."

A few seconds later my inner critic, that old and worn out shoe, invaded the intimacy and began to smack me over (and in) my head. I decided to share my judgments with Charley. "But I'm not even remotely in your league," I whined. "I'll never be equal to you!" His response was one of the most inspiring and timely things anyone has ever said to me. Shrugging his shoulders, he replied, "Equal? Who cares about being equal. Just have fun!"

Fun? Did he say fun? What about comparing and striving to be great, better, best? What about being so good that everyone will love me and nobody will reject me?

Suddenly I saw through my ego's smokescreen, the complex maze of self-protecting motivations. Was I singing to redeem myself from an imagined sense of unworthiness? Was I hoping to use my talent to convince the world, my parents and myself that I was lovable? Were these the real hunger pangs of every starving artist, the pain of seeking love through performance? The mantra "just have fun" cut through all that red tape and put me right in touch with my heart's purpose for my musical expression. Those words became my steadfast reply to the daily diet of "not good enough" thoughts that passed through my brain on a regular basis. I will always be grateful to Charley for the magic words that helped me break the spell of disbelief in myself: Just Have Fun!

In those days I lived by a playful but firm creed: Never miss an opportunity to play my music, especially for new ears. Wherever I went, my guitar went with me. Health food stores became concert halls while I was shopping. Subway riders unwittingly became an audience. If you wanted to be in my life, you were going to have to listen to my music. Friends would call me up and ask how I was doing. My reply often was, "Great! Would you like to hear my latest song?" Actually, it was more of a demand than a question. I was in love, and, like all new lovers, I couldn't contain myself! My beloved voice, served with a restraining order at a young age, had been locked in my throat for far too long. We had some catching up to do.

As time went by I was asked a certain question more and more frequently. "Do you have a tape of your songs?" Eventually I saved enough money, found a recording studio, and made my first tape. A year later I made another. Then another. In fifteen years I went on to create nine CD's of my music. Each time in the studio I learned more about developing my craft. And with every new project, I noticed my voice was richer, fuller, more pleasing to my ears. My singing voice was like a shy, neglected kid that had been given some love and attention. Over time, it had sprouted, grown and blossomed. Often I feel like a proud parent who, in the face of popular medical opinion, had successfully taught his crippled, wheelchair bound child to get up and walk. And then to dance.

How many dreams do we toss in the closet, never challenging the spells of "not good enough" and "impossible"? How many secret passions live within us that are not being allowed to develop because we are afraid of doing something poorly, and so we don't begin at all?

I think back on the years I lived my life with my voice in the closet. I reflect on how convinced I was that I was not a singer and never could be. I'm so grateful I was wrong about my limitations. Perhaps we are all wrong about our limitations.

Say Yes To Your Dreams

Twinkle, twinkle, little star
Do you know how great you are?
Have you been pretending not to know?
Fear has been your friend and guide

Telling you that you must hide
But now your heart is heeding a new call

(chorus)

And the sky is not the limit
If the stars are your desire
Just put your whole self in it
As you step out on the path of fire
Say yes to your dreams!

In your heart their lies a seed
And everything you truly need
Is given you to grow your vision higher
And the only thing that burns we find
Are the bridges that you leave behind
As you step out on the path and walk the fire
God has dreams for you
God sees all that you can be
And if God believes in you
Then who are you to disagree?

(repeat chorus)

The mind says "you're not ready for change"
And the heart says "follow me"
The choice before you is always the same
You can play it safe or you can choose to be free

(repeat chorus)

1993 © ScottSongs

Chapter Three

The SKEPTIC Tank

I grew up in a family that was totally into positive thinking. We were totally positive that our thinking had nothing to do with shaping the direction of our lives! It was through much soul searching and study later in life that I started to take on a most important job: minding my mind and becoming the conscious architect of my reality, with my thoughts and beliefs the tools of my trade.

Like many of us, my upbringing in this culture conditioned me to focus on what I didn't have, what I didn't want, and the worst-case scenarios that might occur at any moment. It's as if there was a character in my mind as grumpy and negative as Scrooge. Any expansive ideas that might lead to feelings of enchantment, excitement and possibility were quickly struck down with a "Bah, humbug!" I nicknamed him the SKEPTIC.

The SKEPTIC believed that life was cruel, and that all things ended in disappointment. He also believed that if I repeat, "Life is cruel and all things end in disappointment" over and over, I would not be so tossed around and disappointed by the harshness of it all. His goal was to protect me by discounting anything that might threaten my reality as I know it. When I was young, the SKEPTIC and I tried on a powerful pair of dark sunglasses. They filtered out anything too bright, new, weird, or far out. They fit so snugly that after a while it seemed as if they weren't there. We wore them well.

On the morning of my first day of high school I woke up with the first of many severe acne breakouts, and it felt to me like the end of the world was at hand. For the next two years going to school was hell, and under the strict orders of my SKEPTIC, I took no risks, kept my head low, and reached out to no one, especially ones of the opposite sex. My preferred extracurricular activity was popping zits. In my junior year the strain of hiding became too great, and I moved myself into some self-expression. I wrote for a school newspaper, ran for student office, and auditioned for a school play.

Landing the starring role in a comedy, I was to play myself-an awkward teenager with a face full of pimples, few social skills, and zero dates. When I took a more thorough look at the script I seriously considered backing out. I had to say things like "Damn these zits! I'll never get a girl interested in me!" and "If anyone knew just how scared I was, they would laugh or throw up. Or both!" This would not be acting, but a harsh reality show of the most embarrassing kind, a cruel form of social suicide. The only thing more terrifying than doing the play would be everyone in school knowing exactly why I backed out. I had to follow through.

My performance turned out to be a big hit. Even more surprising was how much I enjoyed it, and how I felt myself relaxing and lightening up about my pimply predicament. When the play was over I had fewer secrets, and overnight became a visible and popular person in the school. I was invited to parties, given compliments, and approached by people. Even female people!

Within a week of doing the play, I woke up to something major staring back at me from the mirror: a clear complexion! I had come out of hiding, broken out of an emotional prison, and somehow my face had, at the same time, stopped breaking out. What was up with that? Was there a connection? The SKEPTIC, certain there was none, classified it as a coincidence, and gave the credit to the new acne cream I was using. There was no possibility in his mind that the clearing had something to do with letting some light and levity shine on my then terribly serious sense of self. The SKEPTIC was certain there was no such thing as mind over matter, and convinced me to forget that woo-woo stuff. Never mind, doesn't matter.

Three years later I read some books on metaphysics and began experimenting with affirmations and visualizations. The SKEPTIC looked the other way and did not protest, so long as my curiosity stayed at the dabbling level. No commitment, no threat. I was writing prosperity statements like "I am a money magnet" twenty times in the morning and again at night. After a few days of this, I walked onto a New York City subway and spied a five-dollar bill on the floor near my feet. Pocketing the surprise, I promptly forgot about it and went about my business. In all my years of living in the city, I had never found any bill larger than a dollar, but I did not link the five-spot with my affirmative gymnastics. The next morning before leaving for a day of laundry bag sales, I filled my tummy with pancakes and my mind with money magnetism. I hopped on a city bus and took a seat right next to *another* loose, unclaimed five-dollar bill. This time I couldn't deny the connection. I had magnetized some money into my life with my mind!

I began to feel creepy. Could my thoughts really have that much power? Am I *that* responsible for creating my reality? My sunglasses were being removed, and I found the light too blinding to handle. I wasn't yet ready to go from renting my reality to owning it free and clear. I was far too entrenched in blaming my parents, the government and God for my problems. My SKEPTIC, being an expert Reality Estate broker, brought me back to my secure "real world" by dismissing the whole experience as just another coincidence. It was a while before I was willing to use affirmations again.

Three years later I was taking classes in meditation and spirituality offered by Hilda Charlton, a wise and beloved teacher who helped and guided thousands during her lifetime. Every Thursday night about four hundred of us would sit with Hilda. She would love us, entertain us, and then challenge us to look at ourselves and our cherished limited beliefs and identities. She excelled in the art of sunglasses removal, and there were times I did not appreciate her skills at all!

One month Hilda seemed to talk a great deal about her communications with beings from other planets. She casually mentioned that they appeared in her living room and conversed with her about spiritual matters. Each time she broached the subject, my mental "Bah, humbug!" screamed at her. My mind was closed tightly when it came to ET's, and I didn't see how intelligent people could believe that visitors from outer space were available for fireside chats. One evening Hilda seemed to focus her gaze directly on me as she addressed the group: "Do you want to know why I'm spending all this time talking to you about the space brothers? To get you out of your little mental boxes, that's why! There's a whole universe teeming with life, dimensions upon dimensions! Open your minds, kids!" In that moment I saw clearly the uptight stance of my skeptical nature, guardian of my fear, and I prayed for help in freeing myself from his rigidity and opening to my natural stand of openness and wonder. I felt a shift, as if my SKEPTIC said, "All right, it's not likely, but I have to admit that it's possible, as crazy as it seems."

Two weeks later a friend called. "Scott, I know you sell things on the street, and I just discovered two hundred T-shirts in my basement. I've had them for years, and I'll give you a great price! Would you like them?" I politely declined, knowing that T-shirts in November would not sell at any price. "Oh, that's too bad!" he said regretfully. "They are so nice! They have a picture of a UFO landing on the earth and they say "*I Believe*" on them." My head started spinning and I started to feel light and giddy. The SKEPTIC chimed in and said, "Calm down, Scott. It's just a coincidence." But this time I did not retreat to the comfort of my protective sunglasses. Instead, I let the experience rattle my cages and open my mind. I ended up buying the ET-shirts and selling them before and after Hilda's classes. I sold out in two nights.

On another occasion, a friend who was struggling with having to find a new place to live at the last minute asked for some help. I led her through a visualization in which we imagined the perfect living space coming into her world quickly and easily. We mentally toured the rooms of her new home, giving thanks for what we declared would be the easiest move of her life. As we went through the process we both had some resistance, internally muttering, "This is such metaphysical mumbo jumbo!" We voiced the doubts and laughed at ourselves, admitting, "Hey, this can't hurt, it might even help, and it sure is fun!"

Two days later my friend, while fetching the morning paper in her bathrobe, noticed a **For Rent** sign on the lawn of her neighbor to the left. She investigated the situation and ended up moving into the house next door. It was, by far, *the easiest move of her life!*

These, and many other experiences, have gradually inspired me to make space in my head for a universe filled with possibility, one that works both with me and for me as I learn to think in harmony with my desires and not against them. My skeptical voice is still present, wanting to draw a chalk circle around my world and say, "This is your safety. Stay within this circle and everything will be predictable and under control." But I have accumulated too much evidence, far too many cosmic coincidences, to continue taking the SKEPTIC seriously. When he barks his opinions these days, I thank him for being concerned for my safety and I send him back to his room, a little cubicle I call *The Skeptic Tank.* When I first had the idea to assign him his own room he exclaimed, quite predictably, "Only one room? Is this all the tanks I get?" Poor SKEPTIC. The universe seems to be much grander and more magical than your sunglasses can keep up with. Have you considered taking them off and adjusting to the light?

Chapter Four

Phone Service

Whenever I have to choose between two evils, I always pick the one I haven't tried before.

-Mae West

When I was a boy I was quite the troublemaker. I would invite my more demonic friends (an all-male cast) over for a Saturday afternoon of creative hell-raising, and we would go downstairs into the rec-room, although as my sisters and I accumulated every toy and game on the market down there, the more appropriate spelling became, *wreck*-room. I told my parents we were playing Monopoly, or some other innocent activity. We then proceeded to use the telephone for our thrills and chills, dreaming up some of the most clever prank phone calls in the history of the art. Without going into sordid details, the calls usually concluded with the person on the other end sounding very angry and we, the merry pranksters, laughing uproariously. If it is true that what goes around comes around, I was racking up quite a karmic phone bill.

My friends and I eventually grew tired of that form of entertainment and developed other interests, ones that had more to do with raging hormones and the pursuit of sex. As time went by, I pretty much forgot about my days of prank phone calling, storing the memory deep in my unconscious underworld, in a folder marked *Boyhood Adventures Not to Be Included on My Resume*. I'm sure you can appreciate the wisdom of developing amnesia about this aspect of my past. I wanted to be seen as a reasonably kind and thoughtful person, not as someone who was capable of ordering free delivery pizza, Chinese food and delicatessen sandwiches to disliked neighbors down the street, and then hiding in a nearby bush with my buddies to watch the action at their front door. (Oops! Too much information. I must have needed to unload more of the guilt!)

Fifteen years later, my good buddy Stephen and I fell into partnership in a very different kind of phone play. We each collected telephone numbers of people we didn't know, people engaged in some sort of personal growth or spiritual practice. One night a week we got together and made Angel Calls.

Stephen would begin. "Hello. Do you have just a moment to receive a personal message of acknowledgement and encouragement from anonymous angels with absolutely no strings attached and nothing to buy?" Sometimes they would decline and hang up before we could get started, but more often we had their consent. Stephen had the gift of being able to use his intuition to deliver timely, personal, poetic and insightful messages, full of honoring and respect. I played classical guitar in the background while Stephen played the spoken word. When he was finished, he would hold the phone close to me so I could sing them a spontaneously created song that put the icing on our creative cake.

Being serenaded by an anonymous stranger offering custom made lyrics that were written just for them was quite an experience for most of our recipients. Usually, when we were done, they would be in tears (especially the women), and we would all be in amazement and gratitude, at a loss for further words.

When people would ask, "Who are you guys?" we would say something like "We're messengers from the universe, and our message is that you are deeply loved!"

Our friends supplied us with phone numbers, telling us a little of what the targeted person was working through in his or her life. This helped us zero in and be even more attuned to them.

After many months of developing and enjoying our phone service, I suddenly remembered my days as a telephone prankster. As the memories of some of my nastier calls flooded my mind and emotions, I felt regret that my past actions had significantly upset some people on the other end of the line. But I also realized that with the Angel Calls, I had unwittingly stumbled upon an action that was having quite the opposite effect. And I was just following my heart! I wasn't doing the calls to make amends or to clean up karma. I was just letting joy be my compass, and joy pointed me in a direction that helped me heal my past while having fun and being of service in the present.

One Saturday night I got a taste of my own medicine coming right back at me through the phone lines. "Hi, Dad!" a young female voice said. "You can come pick us up now. We're all done with the game. AND WE ARE STARVED! Can you cook up the lobster tails and filet mignon so they'll be ready by the time we get back home?" I thought I heard muffled giggles in the background. Suddenly my instincts kicked in and I knew I was on the receiving end of a prank call! How did I know? I just knew! A prankster can always spot one of his kind.

I responded in a way they were not expecting. "Oh, honey, I'm so glad you called. I've been waiting by the phone. How did the soccer game go? Did you kick butt again? I hope you didn't hurt anybody this time. I'll be right there!" Giggles gave way to loud fits of laughter. The girls were exposed! I asked them their names, and we ended up talking for an hour.

They told me all about their lives, their interests, and their frustrations. When they found out that I was into spirituality and meditation, they got very excited, asking all kinds of questions. We talked about everything from UFOs to Buddhism. I sang them some of my songs, and even sent them one of my CD's. For a week we were phone pals, and every few days they called me with some new topic to discuss.

It was a precious experience, and it all started with a mischievous and potentially intrusive prank phone call. Because I had been there and done that, I recognized that underneath the monkey business, they were really reaching out for connection and greater aliveness. I remembered just how bored and frustrated I often felt when I was their age, and I was able to respond to their hearts, rather than just react to their behavior. In the process I also felt compassion and forgiveness for myself and for my history. My prickly past had circled back to me, and it had been transformed into something sweet and positive. Now that's my kind of phone service!

Chapter Five

A Friend Beneath My Wings

Did you ever have anyone think so highly of you that you avoided them at all costs? There is nothing more dangerous and destabilizing to a low self-image than repeated contact with someone who sees you as wonderful, capable, and worthy. When I first met my angel-calling buddy Stephen I was like a small puppy with big paws, confined by a short leash of my own holding. He played a significant role in helping me grow into my paws and encouraged, almost demanded, that I unleash myself.

One night there was a festive gathering in the *Course in Miracles* community where I was living. Late in the evening I took out my guitar and invited some folks to come into the center of a circle and receive healing songs. When people thanked me deeply, I expertly deflected their gratitude with platitudes like, "It wasn't me doing it. The universe was using me as a vessel." While that may have been partially true, it was also my way of not owning my light.

Two days later I got a letter from Stephen, who had been present in that healing circle and wanted to share his impressions. He wrote:

> *Scott, I believe that your spontaneous custom-made songs are one of the most significant tools for transformation I have ever come across. The combination of music with personal affirmations goes deep into the subconscious to deprogram and reprogram. I believe that as your sensitivity grows, you'll be able to bring forth the perfect notes, words, rhythm and frequency to initiate healing from very deep levels. I see you being invited to gatherings worldwide to share your gifts. I see everyone as having their own song. I see this as happening right now. May I respectfully suggest that, to facilitate the*

process, you see yourself on a divine mission. Value your work, Scott, and more importantly, value yourself. As you see yourself worthy of receiving love, reward and appreciation, so will your work be more highly valued and sought after. You receive the reward you believe you deserve. Have you sung a song to yourself today, dear brother? My love is with you.

Love, Stephen

The nerve of this guy! How dare he believe in me that much! Me, a high-strung Jewish boy from Brooklyn, on a divine mission? Ha! One of us was wrong about me, and for a time I was convinced that it was him. I would see Stephen around at various happenings and always chose to steer clear. When I couldn't avoid him he would look into my eyes with a penetrating gaze, and I imagined his x-ray vision was seeing through my *I'm cool and competent* persona to all the guilty secrets and fears I harbored behind the scenes. When one is as devoted to self-judgment as I was, it is hard, if not impossible, to imagine anyone not judging you, and harder still to let in their love.

Eventually I realized that Stephen was offering me kindness, not judgment, and I was avoiding him because I was too busy hanging out with my inner critic. The critic and I were having an exclusive relationship, with no room for an outsider coming in and threatening our bond. I was rejecting Stephen because I was rejecting myself, and I was getting tired of it.

I began to call him on the phone and ask his advice on different topics. Sometimes his wisdom made me squirm. I remember once when I was attracted to a friend of his. "How should I approach Valerie, Stephen?" I asked, wanting him to offer some me tips on winning her over. His reply took me about seven years to understand, and another seven to put into practice. "Scott, my experience is that the more people think that the guidelines for creating romantic relationships are something vastly different from how friendships develop, the more their sexual relationships will be filled with suffering and drama." Ouch! I was not ready to consider that. I wanted support in wooing the princess, not in releasing my fantasy world.

I hung in there, calling him on a regular basis to show my interest in developing a friendship. One day we were both at the same conference. He asked to have some time with me. We walked outside and talked as we strolled through a beautiful garden. Never one to beat around the bush, he asked, "Scott, you've been reaching out a lot to me these days. I'm happy for that, but also a bit confused. In the past you stayed at a distance. I'm curious what the change is about for you." I looked into his eyes that asked for honesty, with myself as well as with him. "Stephen, you have always thought more highly of me than I have of myself, and that's been too intimidating for me to deal with. But now I'm learning to love myself, and I'm realizing that I would be very lucky to have you as a friend."

We began sharing various adventures. Stephen took a keen interest in helping me get my music out to the public. He took me to Omega Institute, a popular personal growth center in upstate New York, and introduced me to Dr. Bernie Siegel, celebrated author and pioneering surgeon. Nervously, I shared a song with

Bernie, aware that if he liked my music he might play a part in helping me with my young career. The next day he asked me to sing at a seminar he was conducting. That led to singing at more of Bernie's workshops, and to all kinds of exciting connections.

Stephen was always pushing me out of the nest, forcing me to flap my butterfly wings before my mind had a chance to whip out my caterpillar ID card. When my eyes wanted to focus on the ground he would point towards the sky. One of his ideas was to go to California together and drive up the coast on a concert tour, taking in the sights. Stephen had been there many times before, and had many friends and connections. He offered to plan it all out, setting up the concerts and the places we would stay. I put all my creativity into coming up with excuses for why I couldn't do it, resisting a California adventure as if my life depended on clinging to the east coast.

It was springtime, 1990. Network Chiropractic, a group that had hired me a number of times to perform at their workshops, asked me to sing at an event of theirs in Sedona, Arizona. I told Stephen, and he immediately went into one of his inspirational seizures. "California, Scott! You can fly there from Arizona and meet up with me in San Diego. We'll drive up the coast doing concerts. It's now or never! Seize the day! Carpe Diem!!" Stephen addressed all my concerns, and even signed me up on his credit card so I could rent a car. (I had been plastic-free until then.)

I fell in love with California...the beauty, the energy, and the people. When I wanted to hide and play it small, Stephen would nudge me out of my cave. One Sunday morning we visited a Unity Church in Santa Cruz. The service was about to begin, and as we entered he said, "Scott, go find the music director and tell him what you do and that you'd be happy to share a song with the congregation." "That's ridiculous, Stephen. This is a huge church. They plan their music program many months in advance!" My personal trainer in self-promotion was not swayed by my fear, even though it was cleverly disguised as reason. "Scott, it can't hurt to put yourself out. He might take your card for another time. And who knows? Maybe today's performer didn't show up!"

I went to find the music director, who happened to be scrambling around trying to find a substitute for the morning's singer, who had just called in sick! When I told him I was available he looked at me as if I were an angel that just beamed down to answer his prayers. I sold a bunch of tapes after the service, and, drawing on the enthusiastic response of the congregation, put together a concert for the following evening in someone's home.

Time and time again, Stephen lit a fire under my behind and got my feet moving towards my dreams.

Once during that trip we were on our way to *The Inside Edge*, an early morning breakfast club for prosperity-minded individuals who were seeking to integrate spiritual principles with success in the world. They featured a speaker and a singer each week, and this day I was scheduled to be the singer. Stephen was coming along for the ride as my guest. As I was driving the car, I noticed him taking notes. "What are you doing?" I asked. "I'm preparing a talk for this morning," he replied. "But you're not scheduled to speak, Stephen." "Scott, last night I had a dream that I was speaking there. It felt real to me, so I'm preparing my lecture."

"Oh."

Upon arrival, we noticed the president looking at her watch, appearing concerned. The speaker for the morning was looking like he forgot to show up. She asked if anyone would be willing to take his place, off the cuff. Guess who jumped up and shouted yes!

Notes in hand, Stephen took the podium and blew everyone away with a talk about how suppressing negative emotions lead to health challenges. This was life on the road with my friend. Long before *The Celestine Prophecy* popularized the notion of synchronistic coincidences, Stephen was living them, one extraordinary day at a time.

As time passed I noticed a delightful change in our relationship. I had placed Stephen on a pedestal. He was, for a few crucial years, serving as the cables that jump-started my creative engine. As my belief in myself grew, I felt more in the driver's seat of my life, and more of a sense of equality with Stephen. Gradually I grew out of my tendency to look up to him, and began to look up *with* him. Eventually the man who had been my mentor, my motivational coach and my self-esteem teacher, became my colleague and friend.

There is a scene in the movie *The Color Purple* that is Stephen all the way. Celie, played by Whoopie Goldberg, had a habit of hiding her smile with her hands. Her new friend, Shug, took her to a mirror. "Miss Celie!" she said with authority, "You have a beautiful smile!" Celie gazed at herself and began to smile. Her hands went up reflexively to cover her face in shame. Shug took her hands firmly, forced them away from her face, and with tough love caused her to witness herself smile. In that instant Celie caught a glimpse of her own beauty, which multiplied as she got out of her own way and let her radiance shine. That was her turning point. Celie eventually found the strength to say goodbye to her abusive husband and start a new life.

Stephen, you have done the same service for me. You have led me to the mirror and restrained my hands long enough for me to behold my beauty. Your consistent love and support were my guiding lights when I was fumbling in the dark, reaching for a new life. You helped me create a significant relationship with someone I had been attracted to, but didn't know quite how to approach: Me! And for that I am forever grateful.

Our deepest fear is not that we are inadequate. Our deepest fear is that we are powerful beyond measure. It is our light, not our darkness, that most frightens us. We ask ourselves, who am I to be brilliant, gorgeous, talented, fabulous? Actually, who are you not to be? You are a child of God. Your playing small doesn't serve the world. There's nothing enlightened about shrinking so that other people won't feel insecure around you. You were born to make manifest the glory of God that is within you. It's not just in some of us: it's in everyone. And as we let our own light shine, we unconsciously give other people permission to do the same. As we're liberated from our own fear, our presence automatically liberates others.

-Marianne Williamson

Stephen and Scott 1989

Chapter Six

A Gift Is Born

Lord, make me an instrument of your peace.

-Saint Francis of Assisi

In my adolescence, which lasted well beyond the teenage years, I took LSD more than a hundred times. That I emerged from dangerous drug use relatively unharmed and am here now, with (most of) my brain cells (seemingly) intact, is somewhat of a miracle. I thank my angels for protecting me from my own foolishness during that time. Yet, while under the influence, I occasionally experienced coming attractions of the gifts that would be developing later in life. Like divine carrots, glimpsing these streaks of gold inspired me to dig deeper in my quest to excavate the precious treasures within.

Usually, I took along my favorite spiritual self-study course, *A Course in Miracles*, to refer to during these psychedelic field trips. LSD literally made the book come alive for me. (Have you ever seen a book breathe?) I remember picking it up during a particularly hairy hallucination and turning to a lesson stating, "I am upset because I see something that is not there." Instantly the snakes slithering into my space became butterflies. Other phrases from *A Course in Miracles* that were handy to refer to in a psychedelic pickle were: "I could see peace instead of this," and "Forgive, and this will disappear."

During many of these experiences I would pose questions to the universe, and answers would appear in my mind in song. The music sometimes sounded like big production Broadway show tunes, and the lyrics addressed my questions profoundly, poetically, playfully, and always in rhyme. One time I asked, "Why does guidance always come to me in song?" The answer went something like this:

We know you well, and love you oh so dear
So we speak to you in the language you can hear
Some listen best in silence or through art
But music is the language that speaks to your heart!

I began experimenting with asking questions and listening for the musical answers when I was substance free. Over time, as I learned to trust that the songs were always streaming live to me, I found that I didn't need drugs to get online, and also that this gift was not meant for my ears alone.

One day I was at the Tucson airport waiting for a flight, when I decided to take out my guitar and sing to pass the time. Two other passing guitarists stopped to join in on the fun and back me up. Soon the three of us were surrounded by assorted travelers with an ear or a voice to lend to the jam session. We sang everything from classic Beatles to John Denver's *Leaving On A Jet Plane*. At one point, I was afraid that an approaching airport supervisor was going to tell us to stop, but instead he playfully asked if we could entertain there on a daily basis!

I was taking requests from the crowd, letting them direct me, delighting them with my repertoire. (I have been called a human jukebox!) At a certain moment, I experienced a nudge from somewhere inside me to sing *Amazing Grace*. I squirmed, not wanting to wax religious and possibly rub a few people the wrong way. Yet my ego's fear was no match in that moment for the promptings of Spirit, and I let go of my concerns long enough to initiate a powerful rendition of the song, joined by most of the crowd, which had been steadily growing in numbers. When we were done singing, a man came up to me with tears streaming down his face. He told me he'd just come from his mother's funeral. *Amazing Grace,* her favorite song, had been sung there. "Just now when I heard it again," he said, "I felt her presence. I heard her telling me she was quite all right, and that she would always be with me."

Silently I thanked the universe for using me as an instrument to touch this man's heart. I also admitted that I would love to be used like that more often!

Music had always been a source of great joy for me, but it was beginning to show up as something I never knew it could be: a delivery system for guidance, healing, and transformation. I found I could open myself up to other realms and become a singing telegram for people. Often the words would address relevant issues that they were dealing with that I had no way of knowing about beforehand. At the time, I was living in a study community for *A Course in Miracles,* and my housemates and friends were grateful to be guinea pigs as I experimented with this most unusual gift. Was I channeling, improvising, or just exercising a heightened sense of spiritual spontaneity? I had no role models or teachers to assist me, until Michael Stillwater came to our community to facilitate a weekend workshop.

Michael had been doing healing work with his music for many years. He shared his own wondrous ability to intuitively create songs for each person in attendance. Watching him work was like seeing a preview of my future self. I asked him for help to bring my own expression out of the closet and into the world. The song he channeled was just the right medicine I needed to go deeper into unwrapping the gift I had been given to give.

I became an instant Michael Stillwater fan. Purchasing his entire collection of recorded music, I learned all of his songs on the guitar, copying his voice and guitar style as best I could. I even went to Hawaii to take part in a retreat he was co-leading. One day his wife, looking for Michael, walked in on me while I was playing one of his songs. She was shocked to find it wasn't her husband singing. It was quite a thrill for me, to sound that much like my musical mentor.

But I was also finding and expressing my own sound and style, which was even a greater thrill. One evening I was finishing a concert in Ocean Grove, New Jersey. It had been very humorous, and the audience had exhausted its cheek muscles. Everyone was getting up to make a run for the snacks and/or to purchase my recordings, located strategically right next to the food. I heard a commanding voice in my head, as clear as a bell, saying, "Sit people back down in a circle and ask for a volunteer." Before my mind had a chance to debate whether this was truly a voice to trust or a brain spasm from my days of psychedelic overkill, I asked everybody to gather on the floor. I invited someone into the center to receive a song. She spoke a few words about what she wanted support for, and then lay down. People lovingly placed their hands on her, and out of me came a supportive musical message. Everyone was stunned, including me, by the poetic beauty and power of what came through. Other people wanted in on the action, and many other songs followed. When I put down my guitar at midnight, I was aware that I had just turned a corner, and that my music and my life would never be the same.

How does it happen? It's still somewhat of a mystery, even to me. How it happens is not my business. My business is to empty my mind, trust, and *let* it happen. The songs come through without effort. I get a kick out of other people attempting to explain it. In corporate and business circles they call it thinking very fast on my feet. In spiritual circles they call it being a clear channel, tuned in without interference.

My reception is not always static-free. One time a man doing a session with me asked for a song to encourage him as he learned to speak up more in his life. His name was Mike, and he had a Jewish last name. I mention that because when I started to strum the guitar, the music that I felt moved to play was none other than *Silent Night.* That was quite unsettling to me, given his ethnic background, as well as the fact that the music for these in-the-moment creations was usually fresh and original, not borrowed from a Christmas carol. So, in the ensuing moments of strumming the chords, there was a noisy protest going on in my head. My ego was assuming there had been a mistake in song selection, and attempted through sheer will to get my fingers to change direction. But they stayed the course, and in a second or two I would have to begin singing. This man wasn't looking for an instrumental guitar version of *Silent Night.* Suddenly I had the first words in my brain and everything snapped into focus. I started singing:

No more silent Mike, no more silent Mike
Use your voice, clear and bright
Speak your truth and your truth sets you free
To love yourself unconditionally
Speak from your power and worth
Reclaim your power and worth

More verses followed that addressed other issues he was working on. When I was done, I opened my eyes and looked at Mike with tears streaming down his face and knew that it had been perfect for him. That session inspired me even more to let the voice of doubt fade into the background, and to let the songs of creation simply move through me.

The trust and ease that I enjoy while letting this gift flow is exhilarating. My deepest aspiration is to experience that in all areas of my life.

The Call

The finest moments of any day
Are when I step out of my own way
And let the music flow through me
Playing my part in a symphony
Play me as I am
Use my voice and hands
Play me

The finest moments of any day
Are when I'm an instrument at play
Use me as a hollow reed
Let your music flow through me
Play me as I am
Use my voice and hands
Play Me!

2004 © ScottSongs

Chapter Seven

A Light In The Tunnel

I asked everybody, everybody agreed, more hugging less mugging is what we need.

-Swami Subwaynanda

The first time I met Richard, whose alias was the 'D' Train Poet, I was riding a Manhattan subway. I noticed him right away. Big, black, and beautiful, he was busy breaking the unwritten, but widely adhered to, laws of the NYC underground: mind your own business; bury your face in a newspaper; and, above all, don't talk to strangers. He approached me with a twinkle in his eye and an irresistible question. "Would you like to see a picture of the next savior of the world?"

I had no idea what he was up to, but I was intrigued by the warm, mischievous way about him, and I wanted to play along. "I'd love to!" I said with a smile. He took out a mirror and held it up to my face. "Surprise, you're it!"

'Not it!' I was twenty years old, out on my own for the first time, a college dropout aspiring to find a place in the world, never mind a savior of anything.

Every few months I would run into Richard around the city. One night I was strolling through Greenwich Village smoking pot. I stumbled upon Richard talking to a gathering of teenagers sitting on a stoop, captivated by his charisma. As I got closer I heard enough to realize he was using his gifts of rap, poetry, and humor to encourage them to stay away from smoking. Just as I started to turn around and quickly walk the other way, he spotted me. He called me over and gave me a big bear hug as I inconspicuously dropped the joint to the sidewalk and braced myself for his reaction to the pungent cloud of smoke around me. But neither his nose nor his heart chose to register the aroma, and he immediately engaged me in the sort of conversation one does their best to avoid when one is stoned.

He asked me what I did for a living. I told him I was a street peddler, but that I was also a singer-songwriter and in training to become a workshop leader and a practitioner of rebirthing. He became animated and excited. "I've been wanting to find out about rebirthing!" he exclaimed. Before I had time to guess what was coming next he had taken a pocket tape recorder out of his briefcase, pressed the record button, and said, " **Scott, a professional rebirther, will now give a short talk on rebirthing**!" He put the mike up to my mouth, and I managed to sputter out a few sentences on the therapeutic breathing technique that had been rocking my world at the time.

Although he had strong feelings about living a drug-free life, Richard never mentioned the marijuana. He had even stronger feelings about loving and accepting people as they were, seeing the beauty and magnificence in them even when they weren't yet seeing it in themselves.

We kept running into each other in odd places and through it all a friendship emerged. I nicknamed him Swami Subwaynanda, and he liked it. Richard's subway ministry was a big part of his life, and the name fit him.

A spiritual teacher I was studying with at the time warned her students to avoid the subways. She said the vibrations down there were too dense and could be very draining to sensitive souls seeking to serve humanity. I was glad that Richard hadn't studied with her.

Anyone who doubts Jesus' prophecy that we would one day do greater works has never seen Richard raise a crowd of people in a subway car from the dead. Once I saw him get almost everyone on the train to chant "**More hugging, less mugging**!" This was his signature slogan. I started spotting it on window decals and bumper stickers all over the city. Richard, who had once been a police officer in Syracuse, had discovered that he preferred preventing crime with creativity and love to fighting crime with might.

Besides being a blazing light in the tunnels of the city, Richard was also a political activist, a community organizer, a gospel singer, a rap artist, a minister, a gifted and moving poet, and a great improviser. We shared wonderful times together making up songs in the moment, and he was a big supporter of my newly emerging musical career. I was thrilled to have a man twenty years my senior believe in me so enthusiastically.

One tune of mine, *Follow Your Heart*, was his clear favorite. "That song's meant to be **BIG**, Scott! The whole world needs to know about that song!" I had written and sung it as a ballad. Richard thought it was more suited for gospel. He performed and recorded it at his church. When he shared the tape with me, it was so full of his heart and soul I could hardly recognize my own song! He had brought it to life, just as he did everything and everyone around him.

Richard was a Christian, and loved Jesus in a big way. He was filled with a sense of purpose, and considered himself a missionary of sorts. But he didn't share his church or his religion: *he shared his Spirit*. And I had never before met a traditional Christian who so honored everyone else's spiritual and religious points of view. His missionary position, pun intended, was that everybody belonged on top.

When I moved to California in 1990, I didn't keep in touch with Richard. Early in 2003, through the grace of Google, he found me. After an email exchange we had a wonderful phone conversation, catching each other up on the too many years we had been out of touch. Feeling like the prodigal son returning, I apologized for how long I had been out of contact. He welcomed me with open arms, and expressed a strong desire to hear the music that had come out of me since leaving N.Y.C. I sent him nine CD's... thirteen years of material he had not heard before.

Two months later Richard's wife phoned to tell me that he had just had a heart attack on a bus and didn't make it. She wanted me to know that he had spoken of me often over the years and had loved me deeply, and also that he had been thoroughly enjoying the music I had sent. I told her how much he had meant to me, that he had infused me with his passion in such a way that my life had been forever touched and blessed.

Connecting once again just before his death was such a gift for both of us. And now I'd like to speak directly to my friend.

Richard, I will always be grateful for your example of fearless living and loving, as well as the sincere interest you took in me. I will always remember you holding that mirror to my face the first time we met. Back then I thought you were delightfully crazy, and ever since I've been aspiring to reach your level of insanity. You passed your torch on to me and countless others. Help us hold it high, dear brother, and continue to support us in being the light that we are, the light that you showed me in the mirror, the light in the tunnel. I love you and thank you for your precious gifts to me and to this planet.

So forget about race, religion, color or creed. More hugging less mugging is what everybody needs!

-Richard Bartee, 1943-2003

Follow Your Heart

(chorus)

Follow, follow, follow your heart
Find the still small voice inside

Follow your heart to the fountain of truth
And drink from its endless supply

When Moses led Israel to the edge of the sea
He didn't much know how to swim
He followed his heart to the fountain of truth
And he didn't even have to jump in!

(repeat chorus)

Now Buddha he placed himself under a tree
Determined to realize Nirvana
He followed his heart to the fountain of truth
And now he's the East's Prima donna!

(repeat chorus)

Now Jesus he taught us to love and forgive
That's all that his life was about
He followed his heart to the fountain of truth
And we're still trying to figure him out!

(repeat chorus)

There are plenty of lawyers who'd rather be dancing
And some dancers who'd like to try law
Just follow your heart to the fountain of truth
And see what your life has in store

(repeat chorus)

Now some say the end of the world is at hand
But that's not a cause for disgrace
Just follow your heart to the fountain of truth
And build a new world in its place

(repeat chorus)

1988 @ ScottSongs

Chapter Eight

A Blank Check

Do what you love, the money will follow.

-Marsha Sinetar

"*H*ere's a check. It's blank. Fill in how much you think you deserve.*" I looked at the little piece of paper with no numbers, no zeros. Being at choice had never felt so intimidating!

It was one of the first times my music was honored with a paycheck. Dr. Donald Epstein, founder and developer of Network Spinal Analysis, had hired me to give a Saturday night concert during a Network Chiropractic Transformational Gate weekend workshop. Now he stood before me, smirk on his face, as if to say, "Here's your chance, kid. Step up to bat and tell me, the world, and yourself who you think you are." In the few seconds it took for me to come up with a figure, I flashed on a series of other choice point moments, the first one seven years earlier.

"Mom, Dad, I'm not going back to school next semester. I don't know if I need some time off or if college is just not for me, but for now this is what I need to do." Thank heavens Skype wasn't around yet, as I was glad they couldn't see how much I was shaking. In my family what I was doing was unheard of. A complete and formal education were prerequisites for making it in this world…or so my parents thought. They argued, then pleaded, and then begged me to reconsider, but I had made up my mind.

I told friends I was leaving the road-much-traveled to follow one of my own. What was that going to look like? I did not know. How would that pay the bills? Not a clue. Everyone thought I was crazy. I, too, questioned my sanity. Had I just leaped into an expansive new life or off the deep end? Let's face it, inspiration and insanity both involve listening to voices!

I rented a small apartment in Greenwich Village, and sold laundry bags while I sorted out what I had said no to and, more importantly, what I had said yes to.

The yes was to my spiritual and emotional education, as well as to developing my musical and improvisational talents. I gobbled up all the personal growth seminars I could afford, took singing lessons, practiced my *Course In Miracles* lessons, and meditated daily. When I was still in college I had been exposed to rebirthing. My first few experiences with it had been life changing, filling me with a peace I had never before experienced. I began taking courses to become a practitioner, and became quite committed to making a career out of it...or so I thought.

After a year of training I began working with clients. But the thrill had faded. My honeymoon with the technique was over, and I was beginning to suspect that this was not going to be a long-term relationship. One day I found myself turning on the TV with the volume off to check the baseball score while someone was breathing under my care. I had to face the fact that I was bored, and there were other things I wanted to do.

The dream of making a go at it with my music had been singing its way into my heart, the volume getting louder each day. Like many, I had taken on the belief that working in the arts almost certainly meant a life of financial struggle. As much as I hoped I would be a prosperous exception, I braced myself for an abundance of fun and a scarcity of funds.

I started making and selling recordings of my music, promoting and advertising my services, and putting on monthly concerts and musical healing circles in New York. My hope was that the word would spread and that more and more money would come in from these endeavors and I could eventually quit the day job. After five years of putting myself out there, nylon jumbo laundry bags were still paying most of the bills. I was getting pretty discouraged. I started looking seriously at options that would provide more financial stability.

Soon I was sitting in my first class on opening day of a new semester at Queens College. I had decided to go back to school and get the degrees necessary to become a psychotherapist. I knew I had gifts in that arena, and I longed to erase the insecurity and self-doubt I had been harboring in relation to my livelihood since I had left college. I was finding it hard to feel good about myself when my daily work activities came along with being wanted by the cops. Besides, I was aching to do something that would return me to my parents' good graces.

I sat in that class, Creative Writing, the only course I was actually looking forward to. Looking around, I felt terribly out of place, as if I had dropped in from another planet. A volcano started rumbling around inside me. While the professor outlined the curriculum, I tried talking to it calmly. "Get out!" the volcano roared. "Leave the building and don't look back! This is not your classroom."

Being a student of *A Course in Miracles*, I remembered its council about reactive decision-making. "The ego always speaks first. Its voice is always the loudest, and it is always wrong." This volcano needed to cool off and settle down. I took a deep breath and considered my approach. Since active volcanoes are not known for being diplomatic, I was going to have to hold my ground and establish myself as the boss. I replied, "Thank you for your advice, but I will not leave now and I will not leave impulsively. I'm going to make my way through classes today and tonight do some quiet reflecting in meditation, listening deeply and praying to be guided by a still small voice, not a loud and obnoxious volcano. Now go back to sleep so I can pay attention to the professor."

That's when the volcano erupted, catapulting me out of the seat and towards the registrars' office, where I filled out the paperwork for a 75% refund for my tuition. I went home, dialed my parents, and did my best to keep the shame and fear I was feeling out of my voice while I told them I had dropped out. Again.

I was being led, that much was obvious....but I didn't know if it was inner wisdom or my ego doing the leading. Perhaps it was a little of both. What was certain was that a door had slammed shut. College was no longer an option.

I stayed in bed for almost two weeks, curtains drawn, sick with fear that I would be a street peddler for the rest of my life, always running away from the police instead of towards my dreams. Just as my spirits were at their darkest, a ray of dawn arrived in the form of a song, *Follow Your Heart*. As it came through, everyone I admired in history seemed to be there with me, from Jesus and Gandhi to Martin Luther King, all reminding me they had faced challenges that tested their resolve and strengthened their spirit as they grew into their calling.

It dawned on me that I was being tested on essential aspects of my curriculum: patience, persistence and perseverance, and that I could pass these tests by not giving up, by continuing to believe in myself.

The song revived my spirit, and my dreams again had a strong pulse.

Only hours after I finished writing *Follow Your Heart*, my angel-calling buddy Stephen called to invite me to join him for a weekend trip to Omega Institute. I said yes, and off we went. We spotted Bernie Siegel enjoying a pleasant afternoon stroll with his wife as we were parking the car. Stephen, who knew him personally, told me to get my guitar out of the trunk and come with him to meet them. While I assumed they might prefer privacy to a serenade, Stephen, however, had no such concern. "Bernie," he exclaimed, "you've got to hear one of Scott's songs!" The next day I was in front of hundreds of people singing at his workshop.

A staff member of Network Chiropractic (now called Network Spinal Analysis) was there and took my business card. A few days later I got a phone call asking me to perform next Saturday night at one of their events, The Network Transformational Gate. I wasn't asked about my fee, and in my excitement and inexperience, I didn't bring the subject up, either.

It was a very receptive audience, much more active than passive, and they brought out the best in me. I asked for relevant topics and created songs about what people were going through that weekend, using their lingo and capturing the spirit of their work. In response they laughed, cried, danced, sang along with me on the refrains, and totally soaked up what I was giving. At the concert's close, I was drenched with appreciation. They even talked enthusiastically about having me as a regular at their weekends.

It was then that Dr. Epstein took me aside to hand me the check. My head started spinning as I looked down at it and heard his invitation.

"Here's a check. It's blank. Fill in how much you think you deserve."

Donald stepped a few feet away from me and closed his eyes. He looked quite serene, in perfect polarity to the way I was feeling. I didn't like that moment. I wanted someone to tell me how much to charge. I wanted someone to tell me how much I was worth. I wanted instructions, damn it, not freedom!

I took a deep breath, reflecting on the performance I had just given and how energized and touched people were. Having a hunch that my tendency would be to undercharge in order to feel safe, I added $100 dollars to what I felt comfortable with, wrote it down, and handed it to Donald. He smiled, signed the check, and the world didn't fall apart. (Now, after many years of experience and confidence building, if he dared to pay me again like that, I might consider adding much more to my comfort zone!)

That night, my head on the pillow, I kept hearing his words: "Here's a check. It's blank. Fill in what you think you deserve." As I started falling asleep, a gentle inner voice got my attention, speaking with great love and tenderness: *That's pretty much what I said to you before you came to earth. Here's a life. It's blank. Fill in what you think you deserve.*

Whoa.

I sat up in bed, suddenly wide-awake. Was I really given a clean slate and free will to decide who I will become and what I will achieve? Is every check, perhaps every moment, really blank, waiting for me to fill it in with what I dare to believe about myself? A surge of power rippled through me, the power to create without limits, and it lit me on fire with the answers to my questions: **yes, yes, yes!**

Suddenly my parents and inner critic joined forces in my head, determined to shrink my expanded sense of self back to its original size. "Young man, just who do you think you are, thinking so highly of yourself and your potential? You've lost touch with the real world. Now get off your high horse before you get hurt. It's a long fall down!"

I responded by telling them who I thought I was, an innocent, unlimited, and magnificent child of God. I told them either to start lifting me up or to shut up and get a life. They went silent, respecting the conviction and power I was wielding in that moment.

Network Chiropractic began traveling all over the country with their workshops, doing at least one a month, and I went with them. Thousands of people became exposed to my gifts in a short period of time, and most of them signed up to be on my mailing list. I started touring the country with my own concerts and workshops, many of them organized by people I met at Network weekends. What I had been striving for was coming together right before my eyes. After seven years at a snail's pace, my heart's vocation was speeding down the runway and taking off.

Two years after filling in Donald's blank check, I kissed my last laundry bag good-bye and packed my car. I was moving to California to start a new life. I was aware it was blank. And I was passionate about filling it with all the joy and beauty my soul came to create.

The Inside Out

Sometimes it seems your own inspiration is the last you consult
You try a few soul mates, a psychic line and maybe a cult
Then finally in a moment of cosmic despair
You reach deep inside and find there's someone there
And then you find what life is about from the inside out

I was practicing my follow the leader since back in my youth
I went from Mommy to Swami and everywhere to get at the truth
I met a real, live guru, I said, "Show me your stuff"
She said, "My spiritual fireworks are not enough
You've got to find out what your life is about from the inside out"

Well, there's preachers and there's teachers
trying to show you the ropes
Politicians on a mission to acquire your votes
Everybody's saying, "My way is the highway for you"
But what feels right to one may not be gospel for two

Sometimes it seems your intuitive channel isn't coming in clear
But did you notice that the volume is controlled
by your desire to hear?

To get maximum reception from your inner TV
You must be willing to accept your own authority
And then you find out what your life is about from the inside out!

2000 © ScottSongs

Chapter Nine

A Fumbling Minister of Love

If you have an address book, then you have a ministry!

-Marianne Williamson

Warning: Before we proceed with this chapter, please be aware that in two cases I use advanced, sophisticated medical terminology that might be out of the vocabulary range of the average lay person reading this book. For that reason I decided to acquaint you with their definitions at the beginning.

Chronic Critique Syndrome: Also known as *critiholism*, this condition renders the alleged victim unable to notice and appreciate all the good in life. It is passed from parent to child, and can also be picked up from schoolteachers and the media. The disease affects the eyes, causing the sufferer to *anal-eyes* everything and everyone, especially oneself. The cure is a series of emotional and spiritual procedures coordinated to dissolve the layers of anesthesia interfering with heartfelt feelings. People in remission often can be seen expressing gratitude and spreading joy to friends, family, and strangers. For further study, see Jimmy Stewart toward the end of *It's A Wonderful Life.*

Critiac Arrest: This occurs when, after years of a person attacking his or her heart, the heart attacks back, saying, "*Ouch, I've Had Enough!*" The major causes of a critiac arrest are poor mental diet, hardening of the attitudes, and lack of heart strengthening exercises, such as laughing, hugging, and playing.

It was a bright and beautiful Sunday morning, and I was driving an equally bright and beautiful, shiny new rental car, heading to a church to give a talk and weave a few songs into the mix. Just the week before a certificate had come in the mail, officially proclaiming me an ordained minister, licensed to preach. Having been a ministerial outlaw for years, going legit felt good. It was exciting to be less than an hour away from delivering my first legal sermon.

During my years of visiting churches solely as the guest soloist it had been slowly dawning on me that I was ripe for being the guest speaker. I would listen to ministers doing their thing, and find myself fantasizing about what I would say if I were in their shoes, eventually figuring out that I should try my hand at it.

But how to break into this new form of expression when everyone knew me as a singer? Would they accept me as a speaker? Did I need permission from authorities, or should I just...somehow... step in and assume the position?

Of course, I chose the latter.

It happened when I was on the phone with the minister of a Unity Church in Syracuse, as we were discussing my upcoming musical visit. He casually mentioned that, regrettably, he would not be in town that Sunday to see me. I, trying to appear just as casual, mentioned that if he didn't have a guest speaker lined up yet I would be happy to give the talk, and weave together message and music. Crossing my fingers (a manifestation technique popular in the last millennium), I prayed (hoped) he would not ask for a demo tape of my speaking, of which I had none. "Yes! That would be great, Scott. It saves me a search for a guest speaker. What would you like your talk to be titled?" Now, being way out of my comfort zone, I called my first talk *Leaving Our Comfort Zones...* and figured I would be getting some hands-on-the-job experience on the subject.

That was 1993. Seven years later I was excited to be driving a new-car-clean vehicle towards a Science of Mind church with my brand new ministerial license, feeling comfortable, confident, and experienced as an inspirational speaker. In addition, I was dressed for success, and my sparkling appearance added to my sense of pride. I looked good, felt good, and all was right in my world. I was hot stuff!

At some point I chanced to glance down to my lap, and noticed a small speck of dirt on my white pants. When I went to brush it off, somehow the small speck morphed into a large dark streak of oil. As is the custom of spiritually advanced souls such as myself trained in mystical Christianity, I immediately called on Jesus. "**Christ Almighty**! *How am I going to stand up in front of the congregation with my pants like this!?*"

My vexation then turned quickly from Jesus to myself, and a voice inside me began a smear campaign of its own. "**Scott**!! *How stupid of you not to be more careful! When will you learn to pay attention and stop being such a klutz! What are you going to do now? You can't go to church looking like this.*"

The critic continued this clothes-minded sermonizing a few more moments before I asked for a kinder and wiser voice to take a turn at the pulpit. "*Scott, let's take a breath and remember what's really important here. You're on the way to church to be an instrument of peace. What do you want to dwell on, the stain on your pants or the love in your heart? They both exist, and you have the freedom to choose where you focus. You'll be there in ten minutes. Do you want to spend it beating yourself up?*" Not. I took a breath, re-established my priorities, and dropped the self-criticism. Just like that. Without therapy, meditation, affirmations, visualizations, colonics, or psychic open-heart surgery. I just dropped it. I enjoyed the remainder of the drive in peace, reflecting on the ease of my attitudinal adjustment.

Many other times, getting down on myself for what I perceived to be mistakes or shortcomings, I have struggled for hours/days/weeks with the inner critic. This time it was dropped like a hot potato. What could I learn from the ease of this experience that could have transfer value to some of my more challenging lessons in self-love?

I shifted gears so quickly, I realized, because I knew I was on my way to church, and it was part of my job to be clear, loving, and lighthearted with the congregation. I knew self-judgment would be a heavy that would sabotage my ability to shine at full wattage. Self-criticism was off-purpose, a luxury (?) I could not afford while preparing for church. The instant I recognized its lack of value it was no longer a factor.

Then came an inquiry that stretched and excited me, and truly disturbed my inner critic, which is always a good thing. *"Aren't I **always** on my way to church/temple/mosque? Is there ever a moment or place where the opportunity to express love doesn't exist? In God's eyes, is speaking to a congregation any more important or holy than speaking with a gas station attendant or smiling at a clerk when she hands me the change? Is there ever really a time when it's useful to attack myself?"*

That day at the service I started my talk by mentioning what I went through in the car. Everyone was able to relate to my initially making a big deal about the stain, and was inspired by how I let it go. I realized the sermon was more effective and far more fun because of what happened in the car and where I went with it, and that in the bigger picture, treating our stains with compassion brings much more happiness than stressing about keeping our pants forever white.

The Greatest Love of All is a workshop I offer where I share everything I have learned and am still learning about self-love and taming the inner critic. (Isn't it amazing how we're drawn to teach what we most need to learn?) One day in 1995 I was sitting in the front row before the start of a church service. Later on, I was going to announce this workshop to a congregation of a few hundred people, and hoped to gather a hearty portion of them to attend. A playful approach to promotion seized me, and I scribbled feverishly for the next few minutes.

This is what I wrote, though over the years new lines and wrinkles have inevitably appeared. Because it has helped bring some healing levity to the gravity of self-judgment, I include it here.

Before you confuse me for someone who has mastered the art of self-love, I must confess that I have not. The truth is that I am still very much recovering from an insidious addiction that still takes me over from time to time. I am a critiholic.

It is the addiction behind all my other addictions. It has driven me to seek relief from its endless nagging through drinking, smoking, eating, television, chocolate, and working crazy hours without rest. I confess this in the hope my story may inspire any fellow critiholics out there to get help by attending my workshop this afternoon.

Like many others, I spent years in denial. I fancied myself an average social criticizer, enjoying a few mixed judgments of myself and others at parties and other social situations. Then I noticed myself sneaking in a few criticisms while alone. Soon I was waking up and starting my day with a double shot of straight up self-judgment. When I found myself criticizing myself for how much I had been criticizing myself, I knew I had a serious thinking problem.

One morning I was thinking and driving, and a policeman pulled me over. He had clocked me judging myself at ninety-three TPH (times per hour), and my thoughts had been swerving all over the road! He placed me under arrest for disturbing my peace, driving myself crazy, and inner-child abuse. When he realized the full extent of how I had been abusing myself, he even threatened to call Inner-Child Protective Services! And since it was a Sunday and I was on my way to my office, he added resisting-a-rest to the charges. He also informed me that my hot air was rising into the atmosphere and contributing to global warming.

Oy, Vey! Did I feel guilty!?

In court, since the judge knew I was effective in the role already, he invited me to be my own prosecuting attorney, and I consented. Of course, I won the case and was pronounced guilty. With domestic self-violence being such a heated issue these days, I thought they would throw the book at me. Instead the judge let me off with a warning that if I were found beating myself up again I would be serving hard time for giving myself such a hard time.

He also ordered me to visit a hospital that specialized in the treatment of Chronic Critique Syndrome. Upon being examined there I was immediately placed on the critical list. The doctors were blunt. They told me that if I didn't learn to be gentler with myself, my mental habits would lead to a critiac arrest early in life, and that more people in the modern world suffer critiac arrests than all other metaphoric illnesses combined!

I decided to start resting my critic instead.

From time to time I still find myself in critical condition, focusing my disapproving attention on the dark spot on my white pants, the inevitable fumblings I make as an evolving human being. I get relief faster these days as I practice remembering that just as the dark spot doesn't alter the fact that my pants are white, my mistakes don't change the fact that I am all right, and that anytime I shift from self-criticism to self-acceptance I am doing my job and living my purpose as a perfectly imperfect fumbling minister of love.

Handle Yourself With Care

Once I thought by now I'd be
Mr. Functionality
Perfect and complete in every way
But I still get lost and then get found
As I walk this sacred stumbling ground
I want to reassure me, I'm O.K.
I'm all grown-up the world can see
But that is just one side of me
I'm also a tender child finding my way
I sometimes fumble in the dirt
I have a heart that can be hurt

And so I hear a voice within me say
Handle yourself with care
There's a precious child of God in there

There's a judge inside that's sometimes strong
Convinced I'm doing my whole life wrong
So quick to rise up to my prosecution
But as I grow it's getting clear
The judge is just a voice of fear
And gentleness my only real solution
For how can the child inside feel safe
If I'm trying to whip myself in shape
There must be another way to grow
The petals of my heart open
In a loving self-environment
A flower grows and blooms
When it's given the room

Handle yourself with care
There's a precious child of God in there

And so I live life day to day
Some obstacles get in my way
And though I groan I see the strength that's birthed
I still get lost and then get found
As I walk this sacred stumbling ground
But life is getting sweeter on this earth

Reaching out to make heart connections
Making my peace with my imperfections
Finding out the world needs what I have to give
For as I love the child in me
My heart extends so naturally
I can lend the world my shoulder
When my cup is running over
Handle yourself with care
There's a precious child of God in there

1995 @ ScottSongs

PART TWO....
Opening My Heart

Chapter Ten

The Circle Of Love

Humble yourself to receive, before you can truly give.

-Native American Saying

Like most of us, at an early age I absorbed the notion that it was far better to give than to receive, that there was something unclean, unspiritual, and downright selfish about receiving. (It might have started as a clever marketing plan conjured up by certain religious institutions to increase the blessings bestowed in the bowls!) Does that mean if we were all really good and spiritual, we would all walk around giving love, but rejecting the love that others were offering us? Might that be a bit silly? On my 33rd birthday, I found out in a dramatic way just how healing and helpful my receptivity can be to others.

A week before the day, as I was making plans for a celebration, an idea came to me, quickening my pulse with a mixed cocktail of excitement and fear. It had to do with how I had always found it strange and sad that people usually waited for the funeral to express their deepest acknowledgement and appreciation, and not before when it could have meant so much to the dear and now departed. At my party I wanted to buck that tradition by having friends gather in a circle around me, and one by one share what they appreciate about me and how knowing me has enriched their lives.

My inner critic immediately barged in, anxious to crash the party before it began, armed with an urgent *Cease and Desist* order: "Are you crazy? That's the most egotistical notion I've ever heard! You always have to be the center of attention, don't you? Forget about it!!!"

Ouch. I put the idea on the back burner. A few days before the party, I considered it again. I brought the matter up with a different consultant, the wise, kind voice within. As is often the case, its guidance didn't quite match that of my party pooping inner critic. "Scott, your gracious receiving of your friends' love and support will be an act of humility and service, not arrogance and ego. Many hearts will be touched and spirits uplifted. It is only your sense of unworthiness that is feeling threatened. Let that part of you tremble and protest as it will, and move forward with your plans."

Dealing with multiple doubt dragons the days before, I ended up committing to maybe going through with it or maybe not, depending on how I felt in the moment.

The night arrived, and the party was going full steam; people were mingling and enjoying themselves. Gathering everybody and asking them to say nice things to me seemed completely inappropriate, the outlandish actions of a control freak/narcissist gone mad. Who was I to step in and interrupt their flow? Then, across the room, I saw Helice Bridges. Helice is a remarkable woman whose life has been committed to teaching and spreading the power of acknowledgment. She created and distributed blue ribbons that said *Who I Am Makes A Difference,* along with a ritual in which many thousands of people young and old have used the ribbons to reach out and make someone's day with heartfelt words of appreciation.

Spotting her, I had a change of heart, and my enthusiasm for the idea returned.

If Helice was on my team I knew I could find the courage to go ahead with the love circle. I took her aside, told her my plans, mentioned my apprehension, and asked for her support.

Without a moment's hesitation or preparation, she sprang into action. In a tone and volume that silenced a room full of rowdy conversationalists, she called out, "EVERYBODY GATHER IN THE LIVING ROOM! WE'RE GOING TO DO SOMETHING SPECIAL FOR THE BIRTHDAY BOY!"

The crowd gathered and settled in. Spying how nervous and uncomfortable I was, Helice firmly held my hand, calming and grounding me as she told a few ice-breaking stories about how freely and boldly expressing acknowledgment has touched people in moving and miraculous ways around the world. She then explained that whoever felt inspired would, one at a time, approach me and share their appreciation in a voice loud enough for everyone to hear.

Helice suggested that I not respond to people with words, not even a thank you, but focus solely on receiving, on letting in their love. And that's what I did. Two and a half hours later, the last person finished speaking. I spent that time breathing, shaking, shivering, and crying. I had never been so emotionally opened in my life. At first I was embarrassed by my public display of tears, but soon I was not caring at all.

The process was touching many, and tissues were passed around. Sometimes I wanted to say things like "You are wonderful, too!" or "I'm just a reflection of your own beauty." Although these statements might have had truth in them, they would have been subtle ploys to deflect the love I was being offered. Unworthiness can have quite a crafty way of masquerading as humility and spirituality.

Eventually the ritual ended, and the room morphed into song and dance. I sang, "It's my party, and I'll cry if I want to, cry if I want to, cry if I want to. You would cry too, if your friends honored you!"

That night I went to sleep feeling rocked and lulled by each friend's verbal blessing. The next day and all through that week, people telephoned and emailed to share how the circle had touched them. "I feel so much more willing to take risks to ask for what I want!" came from one person. Another said, "Since the party I've noticed all the ways I hold myself back from receiving. After watching you let in so much love I'm motivated to change these patterns. I know I'm going to break through to the other side!"

My birthday circle was a peak and pivotal experience. Since then, I have been much more likely to express appreciation to others, knowing how easy it is to make someone's day with loving words. And when someone appreciates me, I take a deep breath and let it in, graciously accepting their gift. Yes, my critic still pipes up on occasion, reminding me how undeserving I am, quickly throwing some praise back at the giver before theirs has had a chance to land in my heart. What I like to say to the critic is almost the same thing I say to the person before me, "Thank you for sharing!"

Oh, my precious inner critic, I know it's been hard work, trying to keep love at bay. You've gone so long without a break, you might not realize how much you need a hug. Why not take a load off and receive one?

It Takes Courage

It takes courage to directly ask for love
It takes going out on a limb
There's no hiding in your comfort zone
If you want to learn to let love in

It's as blessed to receive as to give
There's no division between the two
And by making myself vulnerable
I discover that it's really true

That there is no desert
Just a lush rainforest
If I'm thirsty then it's up to me
To stick my neck out of my cave
And open to humanity

It takes courage to directly ask for love
Without entitlement or demand
To stop pretending you're a mighty rock
And say, "People, here I am."

It's as blessed to receive as to give
There's no division between the two
And by making myself vulnerable
I discover that it's really true

That there is no desert
Just a lush rainforest
If I'm thirsty then it's up to me
To take myself out of my cave
And open to humanity

To stick my neck out of my cave
And open to humanity

2010 © ScottSongs

Chapter Eleven

If You Meet Your
Soulmate On The Road

If you meet the Buddha on the road, kill him.

-Old Buddhist saying, hopefully a metaphor

I've always been hooked on soulmates. By the time I saw the play "West Side Story" on Broadway at age 8, I was already a hopeless romantic, captivated by how Tony and Maria fell in love at first sight. It was a sight and a love that transported them above and beyond the cold harshness of their world. In each other's arms they found meaning and magic, an antidote to the pain and prejudice around them.

Their story ended in tragedy, but mine would not. Someday I would be led to a mystical connection with my one and only. We would recognize each other instantly and soar into the skies of true love, living happily and harmoniously ever after, flying high above conflicts, car payments, and bad morning breath.

Later on I wrote this song about my search for a soulmate:

Soulmate!

I've been to India to learn meditation
I did a fire-walk without perspiration
I don't need a partner to make me complete
I just want my soulmate to rub my tired feet
I know she's been with me in all my past lives
She's been my husband, my sister and my bride
She sold me a crystal back in Atlantis
And in my last life she was my therapist

I want my soulmate!
I know that I'm whole cause I've walked on hot coals
Bring me my soulmate!
I'm ready to meet her, I know I don't need her

I don't attach myself to external things
I've played that game before, I know the pain it brings
But practically speaking, if I'm going to date
I might as well be going out with my soulmate!

I want my soulmate, to share life's thrills
I need my soulmate, to work miracles
Bring me my soulmate, to go half on the bills!
Soulmate, to develop a nest
Soulmate, to bring out my best
Soulmate, to forgive the rest!

Be my one and only, and I'll let you use my Sony!

1987 @ ScottSongs

Obviously, the soulmate subject had me confused, amused, and a little bit nuts. The wise side of me knew that fulfillment in life was *my* job, but emotionally I still harbored the belief that the right special someone could fill me up and make me feel loved, safe and secure. I had a knack for getting involved with radiant, dazzling, and breathtakingly beautiful women who were either not wanting to limit themselves to one man, or not quite as into me as I was enchanted and entranced by them. I would try to use my charms and talents to win their hearts and minds, but would end up feeling like what Dr. Marshal Rosenberg calls P.P.P.P.P.T. (Piss Poor Protoplasm Poorly Put Together) when they turned me away.

If you're getting the sense that I've had a tendency for codependency, you're on the right track! Smoking high drama in relationships was the opiate I used to put loving myself on the back burner. This pattern was very effective at keeping the Country & Western soundtrack of my love life stuck in a "poor me" groove that kept me missing, longing, *lusting*. This is where I was in my emotional journey: hanging out in an extended and suspended period of adolescence, floating in a romantic fantasy bubble, and on a destined collision course with the inevitable meeting of... my **soulmate**!

I met Alana (not her real name) in the spring of 1994. Fireworks ignited, sparks flying, feet off the ground and useless, dangling in mid-air. Minds blown and heard from no more. A very intense emotional ride, dazzling highs and dizzying lows.

By the summer of 1995 I had had enough, ended the relationship, hit a very painful bottom, and got off the roller coaster.

With the assistance of Dr. Barbara DeAngelis, author of the book *Are You The One For Me?*, I then took a sober inventory of my entire romantic history. I made a list of all my significant past loves, unrequited or not, writing next to names the character traits that I had found most troublesome. Looking over the list, I circled the qualities that appeared more than once, and drawing on the ones that repeated themselves, I created what Barbara calls an *Emotional Want Ad* to help me become aware of a subconscious inner-net dating site (www.shadowmatch.com) that, despite the best efforts of my conscious mind to steer me towards the right person for a healthy relationship, had been doing my matchmaking.

Designing my ad gave me a good look and a good laugh at what I had been creating:

WANTED:

New Age Priestess Princess Prom Queen to cast a spell on me and make me drool with longing. Must be a drama major and enjoy extracurricular relationships. I need you to be able to stop my heartbeat in a single, adoring gaze, only to withdraw emotionally at the speed of light when I get close. Do you like the crucifixion-resurrection story? Let's re-enact it again and again and again! I'll hang out on the cross while you discuss your feelings about the ex-lover that you haven't quite gotten over yet, or a new man that you just want to explore with, or your need to just be friends with me. I hate feeling safe, and enjoy sharing enormous challenges and high-speed heart chases! Come, blow my mind and help me feel inadequate. Are you just out of reach, larger than life and incredibly beautiful? Half-wanting an intimate, monogamous relationship on most nights? Have no problem with very long distance relationships? Then call me now, and make it collect! I'll accept the charges, and a whole lot more! Only spiritually exalted, emotionally unstable women need apply. You'll be perfect for me, and I'll be a question mark for you!

My tumultuous ride with Alana brought me to the willingness, humility and honesty needed to look squarely at myself and my relationship patterns with open eyes and mind. I wrote that ad on my knees. Let me tell you more about how I got there.

In January of 1994 a psychic (who had been accurate with me much more often than not) mentioned that it looked like I was very close to meeting my life partner. During the next few months I looked over my shoulder and around the corner with heightened awareness and adrenaline. Then, while conducting a concert tour of Maui, enter the Goddess! Alana had a striking resemblance to me physically (except she was far sexier), did similar work, had similar spiritual values and gifts, and of course, shimmered with both inner and outer beauty. Seeing us together, people threw around words like twin flames, life partners and of course, soulmates.

Coming home, I couldn't wait to see my psychic, who confirmed that she was indeed **The One**. Reading her energy, he also cautioned me to keep things on a platonic level for a while, as it looked to him like she was needing to have some experiences with other men before she would be ready for a committed relationship with one. That part of his counsel went right over my head, a part of my anatomy I was not attending to anyway.

Two weeks later she came to California. We both wanted to explore the mysterious mutual attraction we felt, so we arranged to spend the summer traveling up and down the coast together. There was definitely a powerful connection between us, and we wasted no time in being public with it. We began leading workshops together within a month of our meeting. We did private sessions of healing work together as if we had been developing our rapport for years, and people sometimes paid us over twice what we asked for after being touched and supported in their sessions with us.

It was utterly obvious that our coming together was spiritually special, cosmically ordained, and a celestial big deal.

There were some minor challenges, such as living three thousand miles apart, and the fact that Alana communicated clearly that she wasn't into having a monogamous relationship just then. Confident that the power of our soulmate connection (and my skills as a lover) would change her mind, I threw discernment to the wind and jumped right in. Meanwhile, I had the funny feeling I was forgetting (ignoring?) a few important things, like the law of gravity: what goes up on this planet does indeed have a habit of coming down to earth. I was also forgetting that slowly is holy when developing a potential long-term relationship. And I was forgetting to take good emotional care of myself.

Alana was as smitten with me as I with her. We were giddy with passion, wildly intoxicated in love, under the influence without a designated driver.

And we were most definitely speeding.

Alana did get involved with other men, and the levity with which I am currently narrating this tale was not so accessible to me then. In fact, I was in tremendous pain. Yet I stuck it out! This was my mate, my one and only, and I would be noble and embrace and endure whatever challenges we would encounter on the road to our destined and perfect partnership. After all, I had asked to learn unconditional love. What better way to learn it than to get involved with a woman who would push my deepest buttons? Isn't that what growth and healing through relationship is all about? No pain, no gain?

What I came to realize was that unconditional love starts with loving me, and I was not caring for myself by getting emotionally and sexually involved with a woman who wanted to experience the spice of variety with other lovers.

Eighteen months after we met, we came to the mutual realization that the wisest thing we could do was to let each other go and have an extended period of no contact. Two weeks into that agreement Alana called, professing her love and expressing her willingness to commit. As words and promises that I had desperately wanted to hear for a year and a half were dangled before me, I felt caution in every cell of my body. We had danced those steps before: I moved in close, she spiraled away. I took distance, she reached out and seduced. It was a dance choreographed by our wounds, and I was tired of it.

When I told her that, she said, "But how can we get past our wounds if we avoid the relationship? How can we learn to dance differently if we just get off the dance floor?" Great points, those, and I certainly wrestled them to the ground before deciding what to do. Was I running away from commitment, terrified of real intimacy now that monogamy was finally being offered? Would I be making a mistake that could cost me the connection of a lifetime? I needed some time before I could respond.

The next few days were intense and noisy inside my head. I meditated, prayed, and journaled. I consulted with friends, mentors and relationship specialists that I trusted. Most of all I lit a fire in my heart, tuned in for inner wisdom, and waited for clarity to come. After four days I called her back, declined, and let her know it was not about her.

It was the hardest "no" of my life. I had just rejected my soulmate.

What I had gotten clear on was that it was time to work on me. It was time to take a sabbatical from my soulmate quest and devote myself to bonding with *numero uno*. I wanted to get a handle on the truth that happiness is an inside job, not the result of a romantic relationship. I was yearning to master standing on my own two feet, the most difficult and seldom-practiced yoga posture of all.

Here is a journal entry fresh from after the breakup:

Slowly, gradually, I have been releasing the belief that Alana could be the only one, that there is only one mate for me, and that I blew it. At times I gently ask myself, would a God of love that seems to have created a limitless universe create only one person that I can have a lasting, fulfilling union with, as if to say, "Here she is. Don't screw it up!" I don't think so. My ego may believe in such scarcity, but I'm willing to bet that my ego and God do not see eye to Eye on this matter.

I imagine if Jesus were preaching to today's crowd on the soulmate subject that he might say: "Seek ye first the Kingdom of your own soul, and your soulmate will be added unto you." It certainly feels like he is saying it to me. What I am left with is the assignment of trust, to trust that by being true to myself, I will be led to my highest good, one step at a time. I'll trust that a soulmate will enter at the appropriate moment, available for commitment, because I am. And the relationship will be like icing on the cake, a delicious addition to an already complete and tasty treat. The sweetness of our connection will feel less like the rush of a sugar high, and more like a gentle, unhurried ripe fruit that freshly falls from the vine.

My good-bye to Alana was the springboard into a new world. When I chose to put myself first, even if it meant losing what I thought was the love of my life, I began to become intimate with an inner strength I didn't know I had. And I told my psychic friend, "No more peeking at my romantic future." While watching a really good movie, why would I want to know what happens next, or how it all turns out? This life is an epic cinematic adventure, with twists and turns that are delightfully and appropriately unpredictable. It was mostly my belief that in order to feel safe I needed to know the outcome that had me asking seers about the future instead of seeing and trusting the amazing unfolding of my journey, one precious present moment at a time.

Alana may well be a soulmate of mine. Her presence, and especially her absence, sparked a deep and abiding commitment to know myself, to be in integrity and harmony with my soul. What can be a greater gift?

It is said that you know you are healed when you can laugh at an issue that you previously felt trapped in seriousness about. Here is a limerick I wrote that brought a sense of completion to this particular soulmate story:

One day through a warm breeze of fate
I met up with a soul kind of mate
With stars in our eyes we both opened up wide
For when true love arrives then why wait?

A psychic I counseled with said
This will be the woman you'll wed
I thought what a blessing, let's do some undressing
And embraced her with both my swell heads

The ecstasy soon led to pain-land
When monogamy wasn't her game-plan
I endured her shopping thinking she'd soon be stopping
And I would end up as her main man

One day through a warm breeze of fate
I released me a soul kind of mate
Looking back on the lesson, what needed addressing
Was I thought we could bypass the dates!

Chapter Twelve

Passages

For even as love crowns you so shall he crucify you. Even as he is for your growth so is he for your pruning. Even as he ascends to your heights and caresses your tenderest branches that quiver in the sun, so shall he descend to your roots and shake them in their clinging to the earth.

-Kahlil Gibran, The Prophet

Cultures all over the earth are rooted in ritual, with major changes and cycles of growth honored and assisted by sacred practices and ceremonies. Alone, a boy goes into the forest on a vision quest. He faces his fears, the vastness of his aloneness, and the mysteries of the natural world. He connects with his inner resources and a higher power. Upon his return, he is celebrated and treated as an adult.

We all face initiations when the time comes to go beyond who we were and become somebody new. A snake sheds its skin several times during its life, and so do we. How do we get initiated these days? By whatever shakes us from life as we know it. The secret agents of change, rattling our cages and getting us digging deep inside ourselves, show up for many of us as crisis and loss.

My biggest shedding of ego skin came through what was triggered by breaking up with Alana. I have to say *triggered* because most of the tears I cried were from a long history of hidden hurts and traumas. Alana was the catalyst, not the cause of my pain.

Along with the grief came the realization that Alana had been the mirror of my shadow. She reflected how I had not been faithful to myself. How could I expect a partner to offer me a commitment I wasn't giving myself?

I wrote this song for the road ahead of me. For a few months I could not sing it without crying. The tears felt good, as they were taking me deep inside, right to where I needed to be.

Into My Own

It turned out so sour
But tasted so sweet
I gave up my power
Laid it right at her feet
I've done this before, will I do it again?
Make a woman a savior instead of a friend
My illusions are stripped, I am bare to the bone
There's nowhere else to turn but to
Come into my own

The wounds of the heart
Need some time to be healed
Though I give it to God
There are feelings to feel
The pain purifies me and leads me inside
My ego is humbled, there's nowhere to hide
I thought that a lover could take me back home
But a woman cannot lead me to
Come into my own

I want to know my heart has the treasures I seek
I want to teach my inner critic to relax the critique
There's a soulmate coming that I'm destined to meet
In my own reflection
I need to know my love belongs first to me
I need to know I'm the one, the one with the key
So I'm taking this time to commit to me
Monogamously!

Now I come to the altar
With my empty cup
God, grant me the courage
To not go filling it up
This is a good time for falling apart
For where can I fall but straight into my heart
My tears are all saying it's time to come home
Each step I take is sacred as I
Come into my own
Into my own....

1995 © ScottSongs

When I first started touching the depths of the feelings that were surfacing, I began to do what I had always done at a relationship's end: look around for short term rebound relief, a unique fix-me-upper opportunity of the feminine persuasion that would serve as a hot and spicy boost for my shivering self-esteem. John, my emotional guidance counselor and therapist, suggested I resist that urge, going so far as to say, "If you do what you always have done, you will continue creating relationship drama. How about trying something new? Why not really take your time with this grieving process, and let it take as long as it takes?"

Take my time? With pain? Use my own free will to be alone and sad? What for? Wasn't the point to avoid loneliness at all costs, replace the loss, and get back on my feet as soon as possible?

Another part of me took his words seriously. It was time for a death and a rebirth. And so, for the first time in my life, I stayed with myself and my season of grieving. I removed my watch and took my own sweet time with it.

My counselor supported me as I shook and sobbed through our weekly sessions. His confidence never wavered. He would say things like, "Every tear you cry is a piece of the past you are releasing, a chunk of old emotional heaviness dissolving out of your life. You are coming alive, getting free, softening, becoming real and vulnerable. It's all good!" I was so grateful for his compassion and celebration, his steady faith that I was safe and on a healing journey. If I'd had to go through it completely on my own I might have believed I was going crazy, tearing up every day and night, with no control over when or where. After a lifetime of living in my head, I had a lot of catch-up crying to do.

Looking back, I can see that process was emotional open-heart surgery. One afternoon, towards the end of that cycle, I was watching a sunset on the beach. I found myself crying *happy* tears, and realized it was my willingness to submit so fully to sadness that allowed me to be so moved by life's everyday ordinary miracles.

Robert Fisher, in his magical (not really for children) children's fable *The Knight in the Rusty Armor*, tells the tale of a brave knight who lived in an ivory tower and who excelled at putting on a suit of armor every day and galloping off to rescue princesses in an attempt to win their love and adoration. Bursting with ego pride, he fell in love with his armored suit and started to sleep in it. One day he found himself completely stuck in his armor, unable to remove it at all.

The knight ventured into the forest to find Merlin, a wise teacher who it was rumored might assist him in getting free. Merlin guided him to contemplate all the life and love he missed out on while alone, separate, and protected in his armor. When he realized what he had missed, he fell to the ground and cried for hours and hours. He slept in a puddle of his tears and awoke the next morning to discover some of the steel had rusted away. The knight realized that tears from real feelings could gradually melt the layers of defenses around his heart and free him from his armor.

And so it was for me.

Here is a journal entry from 1995, when I was in the midst of the melting:

Grief has stripped me bare, alone and unarmed, on a vision quest. I'm getting to know myself real well. I know that unless I make peace with my aloneness, my desperate need will sabotage any attempts to form intimate relationships. I know that if I stay with this, I will shed my skin and come back to the global village with a new, more empowered sense of wholeness. At times I long for an easier path, but I know there is no way but through this dark passage. Ego deaths and grieving processes are part of the journey. There are no shortcuts. I've spent years trying them all, and I found the palace gate locked every time. So now a brave knight takes a time out from wooing princesses and turns to rescuing himself. I grieve for all the life I missed while stuck in my armor. I grieve for all the time and energy I've spent searching for something or someone outside myself to take away my pain… I grieve, most of all, for all the years I was too afraid to grieve.

These days I am thoroughly enjoying the gifts born of my time of soulful grieving. I cry often, and love every minute of it. I cry when I'm sad, happy, disappointed, deeply touched, or tangled in stress. In fact, when I have not cried for a while I check in. Have I been pushing myself too hard lately? Have I been spending too much time solely in the dryness of my intellect? Questions like these, asked with some deep breaths and a hand on my heart, are often enough to help get me in touch with healing tears, which then help me slow down, get out of my head, release resistance, and find some peace if I've been warring against someone or something. As I surrender to the tears, I drop into my body and get back in my heart, where I feel a sweetness that encompasses both joy and sadness. I get to the other side of pain and disappointment much more quickly and thoroughly, truly getting through it, not just getting over it.

One of my songs contains lyrics that help me remember what I most want out of life:

An Open Heart

May I laugh all my laughter, may I cry all my tears
May I love the rain as deeply as the sun when it clears
I want to let life touch me
I want to let life move me deep
I want to let life stir me
From an ancient sleep
Living my life with an open heart
Living my life with an open heart

1994 © ScottSongs

These words have become a steady reminder for me to go with the river's flow of my feelings. Sometimes the current takes me through turbulent white water. Other times through calm, still waters. Always it renews and refreshes, helping me feel more alive, passionately and compassionately alive.

Chapter Thirteen

Fire Medicine

Anger is the psyche's alarm system, demanding that attention be given to a limit or boundary of ours that is being invaded, to an injury or pain that is being denied, or to an area of our being that has become unhealthy. The function of anger is similar to the function of a fever. It helps to burn out unwanted, inharmonious elements. Its purpose is to restore balance and well-being.

-John Robbins and Ann Mortifee, from The Awakened Heart

Moving out the old, bringing in the new and walking through the fire between the two.

-Walking Through the Fire, 1995 © ScottSongs

While I was dealing with letting go of Alana, every once in a while my counselor would ask if I was feeling any anger. My reply went something like, "No. I've forgiven her. She told me right off the bat she didn't want monogamy. There's nothing to be angry about."

One day he challenged me, "That sounds reasonable enough, but anger is not always that logical. It's a part of the grieving process, and can even be useful and transformative, just like your sadness has been. Anger can fire you up to stop being such a victim in relationships so you'll eventually be able to change your patterns and create what you want. And honestly, Scott, at this point your talk of forgiveness feels more like an emotional bypass, a spiritual head-trip. You'd like to sweep your anger under the rug without going through it, but that doesn't work. You can't heal what you can't feel."

I told him I was angry with him for playing hardball, but that I appreciated being busted.

A few weeks later I was talking with a new friend, and the topic was the stuff we stuff down. She got personal and asked me what the dirty little secret was that lurked in the shadows behind my nice guy presentation. After watching me squirm for a few moments she volunteered a guess. "You lead with your sensitivity, Scott, and all the men I've ever met who do that have some rage in their shadow. I think your secret is that sometimes you can be a real angry son-of-a-bitch." I laughed uproariously, and it felt both freeing and frightening. The scary part was knowing that someone could see past that nice guy exterior, and was inviting me to acknowledge a wider range of expression than the one I usually put up for others to see.

In whatever shadows my anger was lurking, it was hidden from me, too. Or was it?

I knew I was getting increasingly bored and frustrated with codependent soap operas, and the fact that I always seemed to be either starring in one or getting over one. Was boredom the tip of an iceberg of rage hiding just below the surface? Rage? Me? A mild mannered meditating man who lights candles and prays for world peace?

It was true I could sense something inside me that was not so soft and gentle, sweet and sensitive; something that wanted to shake me, wake me, and stop me from spending more of my precious time and energy in further romantic trances. That something had a hard and sharp edge, and it was in the mood to slice and sever.

We've all experienced how harmful anger can be. When its purpose is to hurt or punish, it can easily damage the delicate strands of connection in our relationships. But does that mean that all anger is dangerous and destructive? In the hands of a murderer a knife violates the flesh, but in the hands of a surgeon it can heal. Can anger do the same?

While pondering this I took part in a very challenging and wonderful weekend experience designed to initiate men into mature masculinity, a manhood that embraces emotional openness and vigorous honesty with self and others. Called *The New Warrior Training Adventure,* it was all about owning the disowned parts of your personality and facing your shadow with the courage of a warrior. While some participants were led to work on liberating suppressed grief, shame, and fear, my work was about finding my roar and harnessing its energy. With the tough love and support of a trustworthy community of men, I was able to consciously access my anger, and fully celebrate its energy. It was my first taste of fire medicine.

Also at this time I was working with *The Artist's Way*, by Julia Cameron. I found her ideas on the subject very timely to come across:

Anger is a map. Anger points the way, not just the finger. Anger is meant to be acted upon. It is not meant to be acted out. We are meant to use anger as fuel to take the actions we need to move where our anger points us. Anger is our friend. Not a nice friend. Not a gentle friend. But a very, very loyal friend. It will always tell us when we have betrayed ourselves.

It wasn't easy to embrace anger as a friend or a pointer. I was terrified of the hot, powerful surges and urges it invoked. Growing up, all I had seen with respect to anger had been people either attacking and hurting each other or stuffing it down and hurting themselves. As a pre-teen, I watched my oldest sister enter adolescence at full throttle, challenging my father's authority all the way. In reaction, he sometimes used physical force to assert his power and vent his rage. Watching what happened to my sister, I concluded that expressing anger was dangerous. So I became emotionally invisible, hiding from my feelings so well that even I had no idea when I was angry. My survival strategy was to not care enough about anyone or anything to become vulnerable, but underneath the walls of apathy and the pretense of detachment I was as angry as my sister.

Where did all those strong feelings go? Straight up to **Club Head**, a very exclusive (one member) resort where I lounged alone and undisturbed in intellectual superiority and passive-aggressive judgment. Club Head offered but one recreational activity, a game of solitaire which involved labeling and categorizing anyone I felt threatened by or separate from. From my private ivory tower I looked down upon other people's blatant shortcomings and imperfections. And when I would crash from those heights, as I often did, I would drop into feeling inferior instead, my anger turned inward. And so the pendulum swung: superior, inferior, superior, inferior, but rarely could I feel equal and connected.

My spiritual studies seemed to be re-enforcing my belief that anger was something to be quickly disposed of, like taking out the garbage. If even a trace of angry feelings surfaced, I rushed to forgiveness meditations and visualizations to **destroy** it…all in the name of non-violence! I had gotten quite comfortable hiding out in a lukewarm version of myself, a version that had an aversion to anything that could lead to conflict. I played it cool, cooling down all my heat and passion till I became the quintessential sensitive new age nice guy with no backbone for support, a *yes*-man with no access to my **no**.

A scene in one of my all-time favorite movies, *Brother Sun, Sister Moon,* helped me to understand the necessity of being able to feel and express *no*, sometimes with clarity and conviction, in the name of love. The movie was about the spiritual awakening of St. Francis, and depicted how his heart had been opening through spending time with animals and the beauty of the forests and meadows outside his hometown of Assisi. One Sunday morning his wealthy father, furious at his son's deviant behavior and determined to have Francis behave like everyone else in their community, literally dragged him to church, an institution not too fond of individuals having radical spiritual experiences on their own.

Dressed, unhappily, for the part of a rich merchant's son, Francis glanced around the house of worship. His heart went out to the impoverished people standing in the back, a stark contrast to the wealthy, who were seated up front and adorned with the finest robes and jewelry. The anguish on his face showed plainly how deeply troubled he was by what he saw.

He then gazed upon a huge and bloody painting of Jesus on the cross, who, as the story goes, was having a particularly hard day at work. Francis tried to connect to the spirit in Christ's eyes, but was having great difficulty with this image of torture. He had been hanging out with a very different Jesus, a being of pure joy, and Francis felt no connection with the projection of suffering he saw in that portrayal.

While the rest of the congregation was reciting an uninspired and dreary chant, Francis suddenly found his own voice, a bloodcurdling scream of **"NOOOOOOOO!!!!!"**

The entire church stopped singing, shocked into silence. After a few moments, Francis softened, and smiled sweetly. He again said no, this time ever so gently, took off his clothes, and gave them to a particularly hungry looking and downtrodden brother he passed while walking out of the church. He then skipped into the rolling fields and held his own Sunday service, naked and free, the way his whole and holy spirit had inspired him to be.

I love how Francis, who was known for his gentleness, could also stand and roar when needed.

Because my stand is usually about flexibility and going with the flow, my anger can seem like a foreign substance, a hard, rigid rock sending ripples into an otherwise smooth river. While I love rowing my boat gently down the peaceful stream, at times it has also been important to stand on a rock and passionately hold my position. It is on that rock I've learned that being true to myself is more important than pleasing others. It is on that rock that I've developed things like determination and perseverance, traits that had eluded me while I was avoiding my anger.

And it is on that rock that I have summoned up enough outrage to break through into an outrageous life.

I never did get in touch with angry feelings for Alana. But my counselor's feedback, along with the *New Warrior Training*, helped me get honest about the anger that I had been harboring towards my parents, and also towards myself in relation to my patterns with women.

I also came to remember a particular time in my past when I got mad and was able to use the anger to wake myself out of a stuck place I had been snoozing in. Back when I was new to performing my music, I tried my craft at Folk City, a Greenwich Village club where Simon and Garfunkel, James Taylor, and Joni Mitchell had begun their music careers. I was terrified! For the time I had on stage, I sang an original song and also did some stand-up comedy, a form of expression I felt much safer with. When I was done, an old friend who had been in the audience said to me, "Great comedy, Scott. You should stick to the comedy, though." I felt crushed. His comment invalidated the part of my performance that I was most hopeful and vulnerable about.

For a few days I sulked, "He's right/I suck/poor me." But eventually I busted my own pity party, with help from the angel of anger. "How dare he? And how dare me for letting him steal my mojo and dampen my enthusiasm. No more! I'm going to take singing lessons and get really good at this, and one day I'll make a beautiful recording of my songs and mail it to him with a note: "Don't ever put a wet blanket on anyone's dreams again!" My anger had helped spring me out of paralysis and into positive action.

The next day I called up a voice teacher and made my first appointment, something I had been resisting for quite some time.

For many people anger is a place of habitual hiding, a hard, protective shell of righteousness that effectively covers up feelings of hurt, grief, shame, and fear. The stretch, then, is to get in touch with the softer, more vulnerable feelings under the cover. My emotional stretch has been to accept and embrace my anger... not using it as an excuse to attack others, but noticing it in my body, listening to its deeper message, and using it as fuel to propel me forward, wherever my life force wants me to go.

I wrote a song once while I was mad as hell. I stomped my feet, jumped up and down, and laughed almost deliriously while writing it. What an exhilarating experience, to vent all those feelings through creative expression! It was inspired by and dedicated to my mother, the person who has taught me the most about standing up for myself, mostly by providing me an abundance of opportunities to practice.

Never Again!

I'm writing you a song to say goodbye
I'm moving up and on it's time to fly
I wish you and your life the very best
Without me as your captive guest

Never again will I just give you the space
Letting you dump your garbage right in my face
I know it's just projection
You don't mean to be mean
But I don't have to sit and be your projection screen!

Never again will I be your sounding board
When you are using words as weapons of war
From now on I'm protecting
The family jewels

From you breaking and entering the palace I rule!

Never again will I try nourishing you
When it is clear that guilt is your favorite food
You want me for your dinner
Whenever I get close
And I have no more need to be that kind of a roast!

They say forgiveness sets us free
But first we need our boundaries
The time has come to take a stand
And take my gonads from your hands!

Never again shall you take my drivers seat
Now that I've locked the door and swallowed the key
You thought you had a license
To take me for a ride
But you have just been handed down your last D. U. I. !

Never again will I hand you the controls
I take my joystick back, I'm king of my soul
You took me for a softy
All lover and no guts
But my lips were made for kissing more than your butt!

NEVER AGAIN!

2003 © ScottSongs

When I wrote that song I was clearly in the victim position, playing the blame game full out. Although I knew the ultimate destination was forgiveness and taking responsibility, drawing a line in the sand and saying *never again* was an initiation of sorts, something that apparently I needed to go through first.

It was two more years before my mother and I spoke again.

Chapter Fourteen

A Tale Of Two Tantrums

I had written so much about inner peace, balance, and harmony in cosmic terms, when all it really came down to was fallout from Mom and Dad on this earth. What a joke. You think you have a handle on God, the Universe, and the Great White Light, until you go home for Thanksgiving. In an hour, you realize how far you've got to go and who is the real turkey.

-Shirley MacLaine, Dance While You Can

Like most chronic people pleasers on the road to recovery, I did not transition gently and smoothly from being a doormat in relationships to being able to stand and speak up for myself. I actually went through a very explosive stage, where it seemed I had to abandon the *passive* part of my passive-aggressive tendencies on my way towards balance. And the person most often the not-so-thrilled recipient of my eruptions was my mother.

After Alana it became crystal clear that I would need to deal with my unfinished business with Mom if I wanted to one day have a long-term relationship with a mate, let alone any lasting peace and joy in my own skin.

I invited my mother to join me for a five-day workshop at Shalom Mountain Retreat Center that focused on healing between parents and their children. She surprised me by saying yes! Along with sixteen other fathers, daughters, mothers, and sons, we found ourselves diving deep into patterns from the past that kept us from loving and understanding each other in the present. Both my mother and I had hopes that the experience would help us get closer. Much to our discomfort, the facilitators thought we were actually too close and needed more separation and autonomy before we could experience healthy connecting. I left the retreat with the hope that we could accomplish that gently, without anger or conflict.

Not. Apparently, I needed some fire medicine to cut cords and individuate.

A Course In Miracles, my main spiritual discipline, speaks plainly: *Anger is never justified.* I began practicing the Course the summer after my freshman year in college. Recalling that my favorite high school English teacher had been some kind of Buddhist monk before returning to the world as a teacher, I decided to pay him a visit to let him know that I was on a spiritual path. I thought he would be pleased and that we'd have lots to talk about. His reaction was not what I had expected. "Scott, you're too young to be messing around with transcending your ego. You've hardly developed one. Why not go rub your nose in the world for awhile before getting involved in things like that?"

His advice was a bit prophetic, as after the workshop at Shalom Mountain I felt I had to stop studying *A Course in Miracles* for a while so I could explore my anger in peace. (No irony intended.)

Robert Bly, one of the founders of the modern day men's movement, made popular the notion that for lost boys in adult bodies, the key to finding their manhood lies hidden under their mother's pillow, and that they must, like a thief in the night, sneak into her chambers and take it. All I knew was that my mother was still the boss of me (a bossy one at that), and I needed to fire her from that position, to let her go so I could be my own C.E.O.

Not long after the retreat, I brought that agenda to Brooklyn for a visit with the parental units. Becoming aware that I was tiptoeing on eggshells around my mother, I felt exasperated that I was still so intimidated by her. She was saying shaming, critical things and I was pretending to have thick skin. Finally I couldn't pretend anymore. I was at the end of my rope, and felt desperate to break through to a new place with her. It was time for 'pattern interruptus' a phrase I coined for the times when something completely outrageously new needs to happen to break out of an entrenched pattern.

I approached her at the kitchen table, the place where I had dined for the first eighteen years of my life. "Mom, we need to talk." "OK, Scottie. Sit down, we'll talk." "No, Mom, I'll stand." She asked me again to sit down. But I was committed to standing up for myself, and it seemed important to not do it sitting. Sensing that she wasn't in control of me or the situation, my mother launched into a critique of my behavior. And that's when all hell broke loose.

What I did, in layman's terms, was throw a tantrum. I let her know in plain and simple language how hurt and angry I felt about the ways she bulldozed over my boundaries over and over again. I threw out the window everything I've learned about taking responsibility for my feelings and using *I* statements. Instead I gave her a blast of uncensored Brooklyn blame, a dialect she was much more familiar (and comfortable!) with than the California communication techniques I had unsuccessfully tried with her in the past. "Mom, you are the most critical, negative person I know! I am sick and tired of you trying to put me down and control me!! I am grown up now, and if you want a relationship with me, you are going to have to step up to the plate and start treating me with respect, as an equal!" Etc. Etc. (I confess that I am only letting you in on the nicer things I said. For a complete unabridged version, you can consult your imagination!) Something inside me had snapped, and I was letting her have it with all the gusto that I had been tempering and censoring for years.

For ten minutes the storm raged. My mother shielded herself by pretending to read the newspaper. She probably was somewhat in shock. Actually, I was too. But somehow I knew it was a positive eruption that would lead to healing, the way a thunderstorm leads to cleaner, clearer air and a refreshing break from stagnant humidity.

I went away for a few days to lead workshops and healing circles along the east coast, helping others find peace and forgiveness, irony intended. When I returned, I was eventually treated to the following miracle: "Scott, let's sit down. You talk, I'll listen." My mother, having been shaken up by a son she had never seen before, had new ears on. I told her (in a gentler way) what was hurting me. I had never felt so listened to and honored by her. She had been jolted awake and was receptive to hearing my feelings without making me wrong. We shared a few rare and sweet moments of blessed non-reactivity.

Unfortunately, we gradually resumed our familiar roles, and family patterns took over again. Three years passed since my tantrum, and during that time we had again accumulated a closet full of stuffed resentments and hurt feelings.

I was in Brooklyn again, visiting for a few days, and it was not going well. She poked, jabbed, and prodded me with her anger. I repressed mine, quietly seething, static electricity intensifying, clouds building up. Finally I let her have it for several super-charged minutes and stormed out of her house. Again.

This time the thunderstorm did not clear the air.

In fact there was no further conversation, no damage control or reparation. I flew home to San Diego, took a brisk beach walk at sunrise, and wrote the song **Never Again** while completely alone, not a soul in sight. I never had so much fun writing a song, nor had so much fun with my anger. It was exhilarating. I was catharting in art, sending my rage into the sand with my pounding feet while waves crashed and seagulls screeched.

I was mad at my mother for two years. During that time we did not speak. I didn't reach out to her, and she returned the silence. Though I often doubted the distance and the choice I had made, the time apart felt potent, vitally beneficial. Something was shifting in my psyche, and I was gradually releasing the need for my mother's (or anyone's) approval. I was truly becoming my own boss, self-employed 24/7.

Still, the anger, which may have initially jump-started my personal power, was lingering and festering. I seethed with righteous resentment, perpetuated by the re-telling of my victim-villain story, the theme being my mother did me wrong and that my anger was a valid response to her torrid, long-standing verbal abuse.

A Course in Miracles would occasionally show up in my head, uninvited: *Beware of the temptation to perceive yourself as unfairly treated.*

I told it to shut up.

But it's hard to put a lid on the truth when deep down you know better. Harder still, if not impossible, for me to stop the runaway train of angry thoughts and feelings. I had been on the warpath with my Mom for several years now, beating the drum of battle, and I had to admit on some level I liked it. I was having an ego party, and forgiveness was not invited. The anger made me feel strong and powerful in a relationship where I had so often felt weak and emasculated. And so I continued to harbor hard feelings towards her, holding them close to my chest like a shield that kept me safe and protected, one that she could never pierce through and get to my heart.

I was fairly certain that she was three thousand miles away telling a similar story, except her tale had me starring as the villain, with her being the innocent victim of her son's undeserved wrath. We both had collected ample evidence to stick to our stories, and be rigid and self-righteous about them.

And yet she was getting close to eighty years old, and I did not feel I had the luxury of unlimited time to wait until I felt in the mood to give up my stony silence and end the stalemate between us.

On a freezing January morning in Michigan, I finally prayed to release the bitterness I held towards my mother. I told the universe that even though I didn't feel willing to forgive her, I wanted to *become* willing, and needed some assistance to get there. I had a good cry and, in admitting that I had dug my heels in and needed some help getting out, felt some relief. There was an opening, and a pinprick of light entered a darkened room.

An hour later I walked into a bookstore at the church where I was about to speak, and a little booklet caught my eye. It was called *Getting Past The Pain Between Us*, by Marshall Rosenberg, and

I decided to bring it home. That night, while browsing through it, I arrived at a section titled, *Anger Towards Mother Role Play*.

As I started reading that page, the words of an anonymous male participant seemed strangely familiar. He had the very same issues with his mother, and he talked about them exactly the way I would. I went to the front of the book, and to my amazement discovered that I was reading a live transcript of a workshop that took place in San Diego four years before...one that I attended and had somehow conveniently forgotten about. **I was reading my own words!**

That section was a dialogue between Marshall and me, with him taking the role of my mother. He/She listened and responded to me with openness and compassionate understanding. Then Marshall verbalized, in a way that I could hear and understand, my mother's vulnerability, her deepest feelings and unmet needs. Marshall was masterfully using the principals of Non-Violent Communication to translate our two very different dialects back into the root language of love.

What an intimate and glorious shock, to be led to this book the same day I got humble before God, admitted my need, and asked for help. I had found our role-play helpful back then at the workshop, but nowhere near as powerful, timely, and moving as I was experiencing it in written form. As I reviewed it, a warm, healing presence penetrated my body. Gentle tears flooded my chest and softened the grip I had held around my grievances. Suddenly I wanted, really wanted, to reach out to my mother. That felt like a miracle, and I gave thanks for so quickly experiencing the change of heart I had prayed for just that very morning.

When I arrived home, I started a letter to my mom. With a combination of new willingness and some old trepidation, I sent her a copy of Marshall's booklet, along with the letter.

This is what I wrote:

Dear Mom,

> *This is hard for me to write. I would love it if you and I could find a way to be in each other's lives again.*
>
> *I was hoping you would reach out to me first. A part of me has been scared to let go of my anger. I want to protect myself from further pain. I don't know if I am able or ready to take it in stride when I perceive you putting me down and being critical of me with no regards for my feelings. I'm not even sure if that is a goal I want to have. I do know that this not talking is getting old and I'm ready to take a risk.*
>
> *I'm sure we both have our reasons for letting this time pass and not picking up the phone. I can only guess that you feel similar to me.... deeply hurt, angry, and justified about not being in contact.*
>
> *I'm very sorry I screamed at you last time we were together. I need to learn to do anger without letting it build up and taking it out on you. I regret how I vented at you with no regards for your feelings. In that moment I wanted to hurt you, to scare you, to show my fangs after so many years of feeling intimidated. Of course, none of this was deliberate, rehearsed, or conscious. I just blew up and acted out, and I apologize.*

I miss you, Mom! I miss you caring about me and I even miss you worrying about me (once in a while). I wonder how you are and how you are doing?

So, I'm taking what feels like a big risk in sending you this little booklet, which contains a dialogue on page 24 between Marshall Rosenberg (founder of Non-Violent Communication) and me. It took place at a workshop Marshall was giving in San Diego four years back, a few weeks before I would visit you in Brooklyn for Thanksgiving.

In the session Marshall role-played a non-defensive version of you. I was very candid with my feelings, especially my anger, in order to get my pain up and out and have it heard and understood. My hope was that in expressing and venting the anger in a therapeutic environment I wouldn't be bringing it home and dumping it on you. Some of the things I said may be hard for you to read. I hope you can feel how much I was in pain, how much I love you, how much I want your love, caring, and respect, and how much I want to find a way of being in relationship with you without us hurting each other so deeply.

Mom, I want a non-violent relationship with you. I perceive that in our history together we both were violent. It was as if we were boxing. You would take frequent small, quick verbal jabs and I would hold my anger inside until I exploded with one big loud primal punch. Doing our relationship differently might require some work. Do you want that, too?

A part of me fears that sending you this letter and this booklet might somehow make things worse, but hey, we are not talking right now, so how much worse can things get?

One day I hope we can laugh together about all this and disagree respectfully when we don't understand each other or don't see eye to eye.

What do you say, mother of mine?

With Love,

Scott

A week after I sent it my mother called, and we had a very touching conversation. We both expressed joy at being back in contact, along with some regrets, new insights, and meaningful amends. After a few months of lively phone chats with both of us being on our best behavior, I went to NYC to test the waters. The visit was, in the end, very rewarding and heartfelt, but it wasn't always easy and smooth. There were some rough spots, times where we both reverted back to defensive old behavior.

There was a triumphant moment right before I had to leave where she was getting on my case about something. I was gearing up for either a fight or a flight, and actually found a third option instead. I was able to breathe deeply, stay connected to my heart, and somehow hear my mother's hurt feelings defenselessly, her vulnerable *ouch* behind her not-so vulnerable criticism. I offered her empathy, and she dropped into a deeper place. I felt strong and soft at the same time, in my power without the anger. And she was able to drop the name-calling and share her feelings. I left feeling proud of both of us.

As of this writing, we've had mostly smooth sailing going on four years, a bit of bickering here and there, but no screaming, and I think it's safe to say we are now good friends...close, but also autonomous.

We still speak different dialects, and probably always will. Relating to relatives can be hard! But I'm beginning to realize that all we are ever really saying is either *I love you* or *ouch!* And to that I can always relate.

Here is a song I wrote a few weeks after the Shalom Mountain Retreat.

Mother & Son

(Son)

Oh, take delight in my awkward flight
Don't ponder the how or the why
I'm leaving the nest to discover my best
Don't squeeze on my hand as I fly
Let go and wave child good-bye
Oh, take delight in my awkward flight
Your love and your fears weigh a ton
The distance I choose is no verdict on you
Don't battle what needs to be done
A man needs to grow from a son

(Mother)

Son, I nursed you and rocked you
And answered your cries
I looked out at life through your innocent eyes
Now you're turning away and it's so hard to bear
I gave you my all, there's a piece of me in there

(Son)

Oh, take delight in my awkward flight
Let's cut away old worn out strings
I came through your home to discover my own
Please don't let my spaciousness sting
Take joy that I'm finding my wings
Oh, take delight in my awkward flight
Don't pull on the reigns tightly so
I'd much rather soar from your heart's open door
Oh, mother it's time to let go
Oh, mother it's time to let go

(Mother)

Oh, I never knew this would be part of the plan
A part of me wanted to always hold your hand
It's sad, but it's good and my heart understands
Good-bye to a son is hello to a man

(Together)

Perhaps we'll be buddies, perhaps we'll be friends
Who knows where we'll land
When we touch down again
But for now we must fly in our own separate skies
Trusting our love as we say our good-byes
Trusting our love as we say our good-byes
Trusting in love as we say good-bye

1998 © ScottSongs

Scott and Mom 2007

Chapter Fifteen

Finding My Father

As long as there is room in your heart for one enemy, your heart is not a safe place for a friend.

-Sufi saying

"**G**ood work, Scott. Now it's time to find your father."

When I participated in the retreat with my mother, those were the last words the male facilitator spoke to me. Find my father? What did he mean by that? My father lived in Brooklyn, that was where to find him!

The gulf between my Dad and I seemed insurmountable, and had been there unchallenged for many years. My feelings of being rejected by him were possibly my deepest wound, and I had covered it all up with a liberal coating of apathy and pride. *Find my father.*

In his early adulthood my father fought in World War II, survived that, went to medical school, survived that, married my mother, survived that, and became a great, caring doctor who always went the extra mile with his patients. He was doing house calls for his elderly patients right on up until he retired at age 82!

My parents started building a family in Brooklyn, where they had both been born and raised. The first two children were girls, and then I came, the only boy. I can imagine my father's excitement about having a son, someone to guide from boyhood to manhood, someone to be proud of, perhaps even someone to follow in his medical footsteps.

As a boy I was crazy about him. I was the apple of his eye, and he was my knight in shining armor. We played sports and games, and went fishing together. As I approached the age of twelve, however, it became abundantly clear that my feet were hell bent on following another path, any path but his!

In school I was having behavioral problems. I was struggling with all kinds of difficult feelings about myself, and acted out my angst by becoming a class clown, defying any and all rules. To my credit, I was very creative and original in my acts of rebellion. I also displayed signs of brilliance in the subjects I was interested in. But when report card time rolled around, I was filled with dread. Having my parents read and react to my grades was a traumatic experience. Whatever pain I was expressing through my actions was driven deep inside of me. Each time my parents' disapproving and punitive magnifying glass focused only on my poor grades and not on addressing my emotional turmoil, I responded by doing more things that would bring me more disapproval and punishment.

Eventually, I learned that I would be treated less harshly if I did the punishing, so my inner critic came on the scene as a protection plan. My parents saw me being hard on myself and went a little easier on me. Self-reproach and guilt was a prominent part of the shadow side of our family tradition.

My Dad had no idea how to deal with me. My mother expressed her feelings of anger and disappointment, but my father grew silent and distant, as if he didn't care anymore. He acted like he just gave up on me. That was harder to deal with than my mother's in-my-face disapproval. I hated him for that, and expressed my anger just as covertly by also pretending that I didn't want anything to do with him. We lived under the same roof, but we were a thousand miles away from each other.

I continued to have trouble with school until the time I chose to drop out and pursue my interests in spirituality and metaphysics.

I had come to believe in God, a fact that sent shivers through my father's mind. My father, a proud and vocal atheist, had given birth to a son who was doing the God thing, seemingly thumbing his nose at scientific and intellectual matters. While I don't believe my spiritual searching was simply an expression of a power struggle with Dad, he sure took it that way. There were many hard feelings between us, feelings that hardened into cement as time went by.

For much of my young adulthood, I went about my life without much of a relationship with my dad. We had stopped trying to change each other, but the walls remained, thick and cold between us. We had both written each other off, pronouncing the relationship deceased, with no chance of reviving.

But that wasn't the case.

Things began changing significantly when I took the initiative and wrote him a heartfelt letter and he wrote one back. That broke the ice. Many more letters and phone calls followed. Two human beings with a history of separateness began to cross old, outdated borders and to get to know each other. Here is our first exchange of letters:

Dear Dad,

I have been thinking a lot about you these days, and I want you to know my thoughts. It seems to me that in my pain, confusion and my struggle to define myself as someone separate from you, I rejected you entirely, along with everything you stood for. Lately I've been seeing that in my rebellion, I have set aside a part of myself that has not been allowed to develop and that can make me a more whole person. I have come to regret that rebellious side of my personality and I am setting out to make changes.

You tried to teach me, by your example, how to be a disciplined, reliable provider for oneself and for a family. You showed me how to live safely in the world, with a sense of security and structure. You modeled success in ways that I did my best not to emulate. And I am feeling sorry about that. It was as if I turned away from your most powerful way of showing me that you loved me: the way you lived your life.

Dad, I can sense that my work in the world, my relationships with women and my sense of self-esteem are all affected by this stance. I am working diligently in my life to develop within myself the qualities you tried to pass on to me. Ouch! It's hard for a sufferer of Peter Pan Syndrome to grow into an adult. But my happiness does depend on it.

Dad, you are a part of me, and it's time I stopped resisting that and started accepting and working with the gifts you have given me. You have passed on to me a legacy of character traits that are my missing link in my development as a person.

I love you, Dad. I don't want to wait until you are on your deathbed, or until you are gone, to feel and to express that. You have given me so much by the way you work, play and live. I want you to know, as late as it may be, that I am beginning to receive and to learn from you and your life. Growing up is a scary thing, but I'm getting there!

Your son,

Scott

Sending the letter felt like a huge, but necessary risk. How would he respond to such a bearing of my soul? I waited for his reply, nervously opening up the mail each day. Each time the phone rang I imagined it was him. What would he say to me? What would I say to him? Would my letter make a difference, or would I end up regretting that I ever reached out? Ten days after I sent my letter, I got his response. I opened it up and started crying after reading his first sentence.

Dear Scott,

Your letter has touched me deeper than I can ever convey to you in words. I cried like a baby during and after reading it! You have come a long way, farther than you realize!

Scott, don't berate yourself for rejecting me and my values and my world. It was I who rejected you when you didn't conform to what I wanted for you. Rejection is something you learned from me! I blame myself; don't forget, I was supposedly the adult and you were the child! I should have handled things wiser and more maturely.

Scott, listen to me very carefully. Let's not dwell on the past, except if it can help us understand the present and prevent us from making the same mistakes over again. As I said before, you have come a long way and I have reacted to your changes very positively! You say growing up is scary and difficult. Please remember, I am still trying to grow up! Let's help each other.

Scott, I love you very much. I always have! I hope any scars are temporary and reversible.

Always,
Dadio

I read the letter again and again. Who was this wise, tender, approachable man? Was this my father? I felt waves of gratitude and celebration as I pondered his letter. Nervously, I called him up.

"Dad, I got your letter." "And I, yours, Scott." We both fumbled for words, but couldn't find any. Finally, my father said, "Scott, I'm all choked up right now. I can't seem to talk." "I feel the same, Dad." Another clumsy, but heart filled silence passed. We both managed to say, "I love you", and then had to get off the phone. The feelings were too rich for words, but a new beginning was acknowledged.

I visited my family soon after that. My time with my father was sweet and meaningful. I found myself genuinely interested in him, his past, his dreams, and his regrets. I asked him questions as if we were just starting out. We had some significant catching up to do.

We speak on the phone often these days. It's not always easy to talk to him. We are profoundly different in our beliefs, our lifestyles and our frames of reference. But we are two men relating to each other in the present, expressing our caring and support. For my father and I, both expertly trained in the self-defense of hiding our hearts to cover up our hurt, our current relationship is somewhat of a miracle. We are both finding out together that love is stronger than steel, and that the pain of the past can be put behind us. For men in this culture to be more interested in being close than in being right is indeed something to treasure!

The holiest place on earth is where an ancient hatred has become a present love.

–A Course in Miracles

Scott and Dad 1971 and 2003

Chapter Sixteen

The Greatest Love
Of All

Treating yourself like a precious object will make you strong.

-Julia Cameron, The Artist's Way

My career seemed to have a life of its own. It grew gracefully, without much effort on my part. The word got out, connections were made, and I went along for the ride. Many facets of my gifts were getting to come into play. I was in troubadour heaven, getting to travel all over the US, Canada, Europe, and Africa, singing and guest speaking at personal growth conferences, coaching people, giving song portrait sessions, house concerts, musical healing circles, singing at school assemblies, entertaining at children's parties, marrying couples, and performing some stand up comedy. I even did improvisational singing at corporate meetings and events, livening up bored-room meetings with humorous songs about the topics they were addressing so seriously. What a blast I was having!

My personal life was not as lively as my livelihood. Relationship status? Single and counting, marking the passing of the years of my sexual prime time without a partner. I was no longer alone for the purposes of healing, at least not voluntarily. For whatever the reason, romantic relationship was just not happening, as much as I wished otherwise.

One of my recurring fears was that I might be on my own for life. One day it dawned on me that it would be a valuable practice to stop resisting that possibility and live as if this time around I really was on a solo journey...not to encourage feeling unlovable, but to challenge myself to have a full, juicy experience on this planet, relationship or not. No more postponing good times until I found someone to share them with. It was time to stop procrastinating my joy and put it on the front burner.

Making it my business to fill my days with fun pursuits and pleasures, I started treating myself to weekly massages, jazz guitar lessons, tennis lessons, and a comedy improvisation class. What these activities had in common was that I enjoyed the hell (heaven!) out of them. These treats were not for future rewards, profit, serious self-improvement, meeting a mate, or boosting my esteem…I was in it for the fun.

The goal was to be so engaged in having a grand old time that I would lose interest in focusing on what was missing. After all, I knew numerous married people who envied my life, while I longed for what I imagined they had. Wasn't that the game of the ego, to dwell on what seems to be lacking, feel deprived, and chant a dreary *poor me* about it? Where's the fun in that?

I celebrated my newfound commitment by taking myself to the Tahitian island of Bora Bora, one of the most beautiful and romantic places on the planet. Before departing I renewed by wedding vows. Some years back, inspired by one of the many strange and interesting workshops I had attended, I married myself. A song I wrote was perfect for the ceremony:

The One Is Me

Walking with my beloved
Walking hand in hand
Walking with the one who loves me
Just for who I am

Living with my beloved
Living with my best friend
Living with the one who will be with me till the end

And I have found what I've been looking for
Someone to walk me through the door of my fears
Into the light so I can see
The one I found is me
The one is me

Now boy meets girl is the romance
I've learned from the storybooks
And though that can be wonderful
I'm taking a second look
I'm looking at a union in sickness and in health
With the only love I truly have
The love inside myself

And I have found what I've been looking for
Someone to walk me through the door of my fears
Into the light so I can see
The one I found is me
The one is me

The search for my beloved
Has taken up so much time
Searching for the one in life
Who could make my love-light shine
Now I've had me many lovers
I've shared my share of love

But nobody could give me
What I'm already made of

And I have found what I've been looking for
Someone to walk me through the door of my fears
Into the light so I can see
The one I found is me
The one is me

1998 @ ScottSongs

Being by myself on a Polynesian island paradise while surrounded by more traditional honeymooners had some uncomfortable moments, but mostly I was happy relaxing and taking in all the breathtaking beauty surrounding me everywhere I looked. The ocean's warm temperature, clear visibility, and incredible turquoise color were dazzling. It was not easy to pry myself from the water to do other things besides snorkeling.

Coming back, my beloved and I were ready to take our relationship to the next level. It was time to move in together. Up until then I had lived with others, and making a cozy little home for myself seemed the obvious next step.

It had always been quick and easy, the process of finding a room somewhere when I needed a new place to hang my hat. At the end of one of my local concerts I'd make an announcement that I was looking for a new living situation and someone would let me know they were looking for a new housemate. I wasn't choosy, and if the universe served it on my plate, I figured it was meant to be. I fancied myself quite adept at going with the flow.

Looking back on it, I suspect this easy-going attitude was in part springing from a leak in my self-loving; I didn't feel deserving enough to envision something I really wanted, put my order out, and possibly receive it. Instead, I watered down my desires, took what was offered, and lived with whatever came along.

It's said that beggars can't be choosers, and I was ready to throw off my beggar identity and choose a dwelling that made me tingle and soar. I was ready to take a big leap in self-nurturing, much like learning to cook gourmet meals for oneself after years of resorting to the microwave.

I began searching for my new home by getting clear on what I wanted and writing it down. I spent some time each morning meditating on the following wish list:

My Ideal Living Space

1. Within walking distance of the beach.

2. Tucked away in nature, surrounded by abundant greenery, quiet and peaceful, yet five minutes or less from civilization.

3. A lovely cottage type of place, with bedroom, kitchen, office space, living room, and a nice bathroom with a bathtub shower with good water pressure.

4. Good sun exposure, bright and cheerful.

5. Freedom to make plenty of noise musically and emotionally.

6. Plenty of storage space for my CD's and other stuff.

7. The rent is $800 or less and the landlord is very nice, helpful and cooperative.

8. There is a cozy backyard, nice greenery with an abundance of sun.

9. The space has a feeling of a sanctuary. It feels safe, peaceful, and exciting to live there.

This or something better now manifests for me by the first of November. Thank you God for this beautiful living space.

Now, besides covering all my metaphysical bases by visualizing myself residing there and giving thanks for my wonderful new home, I was also bringing my vision down to earth by telling everyone I knew exactly what I was looking for and asking for their support, scouring the newspapers for ads (this was pre-Craig list), and driving around my favorite neighborhoods in search of *For Rent* signs.

Several places I visited were quite tempting. One place had everything I wanted except adequate sunlight. Another was perfect except that it was on a street with traffic noise. One was so close to my dream that I even went so far as to write out a check to hold my place, but the next day woke up and had to admit that it, too, was not quite *the one.*

What was happening to me? Would any place be good enough for my impossibly high standards? Maybe I was becoming a snob. Three months of courting close calls had gone by, and I was getting pretty frustrated. One day, while driving away from another near miss, I noticed I was starting to feel weak in terms of my sobriety.

What began as one glass of whine rapidly became thinking the hard stuff. *What's wrong with me? Am I screwing things up? God, why are you withholding from me? Am I being punished? Is this my karma? Should I just take any old place and be done with it?"*

Weary of where these kinds of leading questions were leading, I decided to ask a few others, ones that did not keep me wandering down the victim trail: *"What soul qualities might I be developing by having this search take longer than I want? What gifts can the universe be conspiring to bless me with through this experience?"* Sometimes the right questions turn everything around. A one-word answer rippled down my spine, instantly causing my relapse to relax and the grievance my ego had placed before God to release. *Patience.*

Ah, patience. What was that? And where could I get some right away? Much of my life I seemed to be on a quest for instant gratification. Looking at my wish list, I saw that it needed revising. Where I had written, "This or something better now manifests for me by the first of November", I changed it to: "This or something better now manifests for me *in God's perfect timing* for the highest good of all." My goal changed from getting my dream-place as quickly as possible, to having peace and patience with the process of finding it.

It was as if my inner child had been jumping up and down, shouting "I must have it now, and I refuse to be peaceful until I get it!" We had a chat, my child-self and I, in which I let him rant and rave and vent. All I did was validate his feelings. After being listened to with compassion, he was willing to listen to my adult-self, and I coached him on how much more fun we could have if we weren't so outcome oriented. There was a discernable shift, and I felt both excited and at ease about the grand adventure of finding an ideal home, however long it took.

Two weeks after I emotionally let go of my attachment to when I would find it, the perfect place showed up.

Following up on an ad in a paper for a one-bedroom guesthouse, I walked into a charming cottage-type of place in my favorite neighborhood in Encinitas, a five-minute walk to the beach. It met all the essentials on my list and then some. If I were a hand, this was my glove, and it fit perfectly. I imagined the writing I would do in it. I imagined how I would furnish it. I imagined filling the space with warm, loving energy. My head was buzzing as I filled out an application alongside many other people, some of them like me, drooling with desire. This place was a rare find.

I went home and waited (not-so patiently) for the phone to ring while I petitioned the universe with prayer, visualization, and some traditional begging. The next day I heard from my new (you can see I practice positive thinking) landlord. "We've offered the place to a woman who's not sure if she's going to take it; she'll be letting us know later on today. If she declines, you're next in line. Do you still want in?"

I spent a few hours walking along the beach, surfing a wild range of emotions, including waves of anxiety, which came up strongly as I allowed myself to feel my juice for this place. I realized why I had spent much of my life not going for the gold. Mediocrity was a safe haven from the fear of loss. The beach was unusually deserted that December day, and I was able to shout my thoughts and feelings out to God, trembling out my fears of not getting it, while affirming my faith that I was being led to my highest good, and that if this wasn't the place, it would be something better.

The call that afternoon was good news, and two weeks later I moved in.

I lived in that cozy cottage for seven glorious years, and wrote the bulk of this book there. I adored the fruit trees outside my window: avocado, apple, orange, even peach. Besides feasting on free fruit, I also enjoyed a delicious sense of satisfaction, knowing that I had leaped far from the confines of my comfort zone to manifest a perfect home for that stage of my life.

Slowly and gradually, I settled in to my new pad. For the first time in my life, I picked out and bought my own furniture and other decorum. While furnishing my new home, I felt myself relax and sink more deeply into the earth. For someone who had specialized in *routes, roots* were an awesome addition.

I started most days with a beach walk, communing and connecting both with nature and with my inner child. I practiced replacing the inner critic's endless parade of judgments with affirmative, uplifting self-talk. I bought myself fresh flowers each week, and wrote daily gratitudes and love notes to myself in my journal.

There is a popular song from the 1980's proclaiming self-love is... *The Greatest Love of All.* I'm not sure if I agree with that, as I prefer to think that all love is created equal, but certainly I was experiencing firsthand how crucial and sweet it is to be loved by me. A daily practice of loving myself helped build the foundation I never had, the roots under my feet that made for some wonderful branching out. Being on my own, previously experienced as a hardship to either be avoided or endured, was becoming something magnificent and healing…a pathway home to my soul.

A journal entry from the third month in the cottage says it all:

Here I am now, completing another ordinary day in my life. Before sitting down to write this I did my laundry, folding it with care and love. Before that I went food shopping, made lunch, and took a quiet walk. To the thrill seeking part of me, it all sounds so dull, and yet I am loving these days, the very kind I used to find frustrating and boring. I relish this feeling of being at home inside my skin, not keeping my eyes constantly peeled for someone to fall in love with, but just keeping myself good company and appreciating life exactly as it is. I think I have finally come to value having my feet on the ground more than a ride on relationship's rollercoaster. And for that I am extraordinarily relieved and grateful.

The Flight Of The Tree

Ever since I was a little boy
My heart would dream of flight
From the tears I shed I would take my jet
Trying to soar into the light
Well, I made it to the sky most times
Taking in the view I found
But the tears would come back to my eyes
When I crashed back on the ground

At the point of being on my knees
With no runway left to turn
I came face to face with an oak tree
And a mighty truth to learn
I said, "Oak tree, my, how high you've grown
What a point of view you've found"
It said, "What sustains my soaring heights
Are my roots deep in the ground"

Out of my mouth there came a prayer
Like I never prayed before
For my words had power from my pain
And it shook me to my core
I said, "Mother earth and father sky
There's a lesson here for me
For from birth I've dreamed that I can fly
Without rooting like this tree"

Plant my feet in soil firm and high
To the earth I must return
For although I might be born to fly
There's some groundwork here to learn
So I let my spirit sink back in
To the soil I feared would hurt
And I found my soul could really grow
In the middle of the dirt

As for the rest, you know it well
For it's what all life's about
As my roots grew stronger in the ground

I began my branching out
Tall and thick and full of heart
How I'm growing like a tree
But I won't forget how I got my start
Being wounded on my knees

And when heaven's winds blow through my leaves
I give thanks for my rebirth
For the flight I yearned for was conceived
The day I came back to earth

1998 @ ScottSongs

Chapter Seventeen

Revisiting

Roller Coasters

Soul mates are forged, not found.

-Jett Psaris and Marlena Lyons

"You know, I'm really attracted to you and if you lived closer I'd ask you out on a date."*

"You know, Scott, I feel the same way."

An awkward but sweet moment.

I was having dinner with an old acquaintance of mine after spending a lovely day together in Santa Cruz. Our exchange of heartfelt words touched me, but I was also feeling well protected, safe and secure behind my rule against getting involved with any women who lived far away.

I wasn't quite prepared when this lovely lady, Venus by name, called a few days later to say she really wanted us to spend some time getting to know each other better. My response was a speech about the evils of long distance dating, and how it was like buying a ticket for a roller coaster of longing and drama, one with far fewer ups than downs. I emphasized that I'd been there and done that already and for the last time, thank you.

"So, Scott," she said, "is that your highest truth or are you just venting?"

Both impressed and thrown off balance by the piercing simplicity of her question, I was anxious to impress her back by responding with some clarity of my own. None came. After a deafening silence, I finally sputtered out, "I'll have to get back to you on that one."

This woman and the dilemma she presented had me both enthused and confused. It had been six years since we had seen each other last. And it had been thirteen years since I had first laid eyes on her. Venus had been twenty-one then, eight years my junior, when she came with her mother to one of my concerts. I was drawn to her immediately, but whenever I tried to make eye contact she looked away.

Venus became a regular at my concerts and workshops. My ego enjoyed having this beautiful young woman looking up at me as though I was very evolved, a spiritual superstar, but I knew a romantic relationship, although perhaps a fun subject for my fantasies, was out of the question. Sooner or later pedestals like that come crashing down, and the crash is painful for everyone.

Then she moved 500 miles away and that was that. I didn't see or hear from her for another six years until one day she emailed me to buy my children's CD for her nieces and nephews. I saw her address and in my reply mentioned that I would be speaking soon a few hours from where she lived. I invited her to the talk and then lunch with me afterwards. She came, and lunch evolved into a magical beach walk, and then stretched on into dinner.

In those six years Venus had gone from a student and a fan, to a powerful woman comfortable and at ease in her own skin. Our conversations were full of depth, warmth, honesty, and levity. She had grown so much in such a short period of time, and I enjoyed and appreciated the person she had become.

Back home, I started reconsidering this *never again* policy on long distance dating. Hearing the still, small voice of intuitive guidance can be hard when stuffed up with noisy, rigid rules, and I wrestled with whether the reappearance of Venus was a test of my resolve to stay true to my boundaries, or an invitation to loosen them up and get to know someone better who really interested me. Curiously enough, Venus had already made plans to visit a friend who lived near me the following weekend, and was going to have some free time. The stage was set. I decided to see her again.

She had recently posted a Match.com ad, and towards the end of our delightful second visit she read it to me. She asked if it was an ad I would consider responding to. It read:

I am a seeker in the spiritual sense. I love to learn, laugh, explore, change, and I desire to grow forever. I am mostly interested in finding that place of peace inside myself regardless of my life situation. I am in recovery from the disease of spiritual seriousness and am learning that life is meant to be enjoyed and it is really OK to have fun for the sake of having fun. I love people, and am learning that all judgments I have of others are really about... oops... me.

I am committed to self-responsibility, finding my own joy, laughing at life, healthy eating, honoring the earth, kindness, generosity, exercise, doing what I love, following my heart, being courageous, finding what is right with everything and creating anything out of nothing. I desire to travel, explore, teach healing and transformation, challenge myself and be challenged by you.

You are kind, generous, playful, open-minded, have your own life, self-aware and self-responsible, want me to be your best friend, want a family with me, and desire to grow forever. We don't need each other; we simply choose daily to share our life and our love together. You are open to being loved fully and are ready to be seen, held, adored, cherished, challenged, and heated up. You are passionate, very creative in bed, love to snuggle-public displays of affection get special rewards. You take responsibility for your feelings and needs and are not afraid of them.

I will not let you hide in old patterns. I will demand the best of you and ask you to do the same for me. Are you ready for the ultimate adventure? The journey of self-discovery that opens doors to intimacy that neither of us knew existed? Together we will explore the full range of human expression, laugh ourselves silly, create new things, make love with abandon, cry in each others arms and celebrate the tenuousness of life with a grace that flows easily.

Wow! I struggled to keep my cool in the midst of some major heart palpitations. Part of me wanted to jump up and down and shout, "I've met my match!" Another part of me urged caution. "Words are just words. Time will tell who this person is and who we might be to each other. And having a child? That's the biggest life changer of them all, a huge decision, and I would need to be crystal clear before going there."

Both the celebration and caution seemed a natural mix at the start of a friendship. And I was certain that it was friendship I wanted first, before anything else could develop. In earlier relationships I had tried to get intimate as soon as possible, and I had intimate knowledge of the trouble that followed. I read somewhere that a soulmate is a best friend you eventually get sexy with. I never had a best friend and lover in one person, and I wanted to see if that was possible with Venus. I became a big advocate for taking our time, savoring each step of the process, and for building lots of safety and trust before getting physical.

On our third visit Venus let me know that she had also gone through a huge and very painful breakup, and had a major transformation during the grieving of it at just about the same time that I had. Like me, she had then also taken time away from romantic relationships to learn to enjoy her own company more thoroughly, and to really get that she was a whole and complete person with or without a partner.

She told me about her past patterns, growing pains and lessons learned from her entire romantic and sexual history. Her Dad had died when she was still a child, and as an adult she had been drawn to men who appeared strong and stable on the outside, holding out the hope and promise of filling the Daddy void, but at the end of the dating day, as the initial high faded, they turned out to be terrified of intimacy, emotionally shut down, and controlling. She told me all this as if to say, "Hey, if you are going to be anything like my past lovers, I want to smoke you out now. Come clean, and save us both the head and heartaches." I chose a musical way of assuring her I was not in that category. The song also served as a test to see if she could be lighthearted about the shadow side of what she had been creating. She laughed throughout the song, and even ended up singing background vocals on it six months later when I recorded it professionally.

Mr. Right

Venus:

My Mr. Right has just arrived
At last I get to be a bride
No more wishing, no more waiting
No more awkward dot-com dating
He's tall and dark and beyond cute
So shining in his armored suit
He's my white knight, a total charmer
My love will melt off all that armor

Scott:

Hello sweet thing I am your perfect man
Your search is over start the wedding plans
I will take care of you so do not fear
Just clean the house and fetch me one more beer

I am your soul mate, call me Mr. Right
I make good money and my teeth are white
I've got the confidence you wish you had
I'll treat you swell if you don't make me mad

The first few months I'll sweep you off your feet
I'll take you out for tasty things to eat
Then when we're steady you will come to know
Just what is underneath my machismo

I've got an inner child that loves to whine
He needs his Momma's breast but yours will do fine
I throw a tantrum when I don't get my way
And if the truth be known, I think I might be gay

You like my muscles, I was made to win
I work out everything right in the gym
I will protect you, you are in good hands
If you play helpless I'll play Superman

The time goes by and something isn't right
We're watching DVD's most every night
You want to talk about your feelings again
While I'm fantasizing about your best friend

Goodbye sweet thing just call me Mr. Wrong
For you have wised up and have said, so long
I had you fooled until you finally discovered
You can't judge a man just by reading his cover

So off I go to find my next conquest
While you get busy on your consciousness
You learn some self-respect and dignity
So you won't search for Daddy in guys like me

The human race it seems will go on mating
There ain't no future in just masturbating
You'll find your happiness without a mate
And then meet a man with no 'S' on his cape

2004 @ ScottSongs

Throughout our getting to know each other, we were both aware of huge potentials stirring between us. Yet there were a variety of things to work on, work out, and grapple with. Like the child conversation, for instance.

Venus came to the table with a clear and non-negotiable desire for a baby. I came to the table tipping with uncertainty about having children, or anything else that might add weight to my plate. I liked traveling light, my life improvised and unplanned. She, however, was dealing with a biological clock that had begun sounding its alarm well before we began dating.

Venus loved to talk about the things we could do together-workshops we could teach, countries we could visit, and the joys of creating a truly functional and happy family. In return, I lectured her on the necessity of coming back from the future and being here now, quoting Eckhart Tolle and Ram Dass to make my case. I may have had some good points, but really I was just trying to control her and get my way. My manipulative tendencies came packaged in spiritual vocabulary, that's all, and all of it was my best attempt to slow things down so I could feel less afraid and less, well, *out of control.*

Becoming a parent had not seriously entered my mind until Venus entered my orbit. I needed time to consider it. How much time? A few decades! Frankly, it scared me beyond any willingness to talk about it. I shut down around the baby conversation, and tried to shut her down as well. It wasn't that I was completely closed to parenthood; it was just that I was a freedom-loving/responsibility-phobic guy with an extensive collection of unexamined and unchallenged fears showing up in my face. Taking it slowly was my strategy for managing being overwhelmed, and dealing with my fears in bite-sized chunks. I wanted baby steps, while Venus wanted leaps (and babies).

At some point almost every couple faces at least one seemingly insurmountable obstacle, a potential deal breaker that creates tremendous friction, and can spark plenty of growth and healing as well. This was surely ours.

Venus grumbled (and occasionally growled) in frustration over my control issues and yet, even when my ego attempted to throw her, stayed on the horse. Early on in our dating an inner voice she trusted told her I would eventually be her life partner and father of her child. She was wise enough to not share that with me, to let me go through my doubts and struggles along the way without unsolicited prophecy.

Not that her own faith was unwavering. She had doubts as well, and was not shy about letting me know exactly what they were. Determined not to behave in a prescribed way to please and keep her guy, Venus was passionate about speaking up about difficult things, even if it meant me getting angry, or even leaving. It was one of the things about her that attracted me, while at the same time challenging me deeply.

She voiced her concerns about the sloppy, unstylish way I dressed, how childish I sometimes seemed to her, and questioned whether I was enough of a man so that she could be my partner, and not morph into being my parent. She had a problem with my constant kidding around, and was having a hard time developing trust when I was so often the trickster. My reactions to all this ranged from getting defensive and angry, to realizing that some of the things she was having a problem with were things that would benefit me to change... the constant kidding around, for instance, as well as the hippie clothes from my psychedelic twenties. There were definitely some aspects of my life I was ready to clear out.

Neither of us was interested in putting our best foot forward and being good little "dates". We put both feet forward right off the bat, testing each other to see if truth telling and transparency were welcome. There is a book by Kyle King titled *Truth First, Love Second, For The Truth is Love's Doorway*. And so, we forged a rugged pathway to true love, one truth at a time. One of my songs contains these lyrics:

Sometimes your truth might rock the boat
But boats were made for rocking
A summer storm will get you soaked
But when the storm is through
You feel totally brand new

Early on we took this (relation)ship out of the harbor and out to sea. With my newfound commitment to myself as my first and sometimes only priority, I wasn't always considerate of how I came across to Venus. In fact, I was occasionally quite dictatorial as I laid out my rules, needs, and boundaries, sometimes as if her feelings didn't matter. Let's see, there was no kissing for three months, no sex for another three, no talking more than every other day, and no coming to my gigs while we were dating.

And what was up with that last one? I wanted to make sure that I wasn't going to charm and manipulate her with my talents. Does that sound silly and extreme? I had tried that with every woman who came before, and it was important to me not to go there again. I thank my lucky stars that planet Venus, although not happy with all the rigid rules, stayed with me while I eventually and ever so gradually learned to surrender the protection plan that had been so carefully layered over my heart.

Songwriting, as always, was my finest therapy, helping me soothe and sort through all the mixed feelings I was having.

My head is in a spin
How do I let you in
And not give up on me
That's my priority

I'd rather tell you no
And risk having you go
Than be your shining knight
In armor that's too tight

After a year of long distance I moved to Marin County, California to be close to Venus. I got my own place in her neighborhood, willing at least to share a zip code. It took yet another two years before I was ready to share a whole address. And so, for the first time in my life I wasn't dreaming and pining for an intimate other. My sweetie was right down the road, available, non-smothering, reasonably balanced and sane.

What was next for me in our love story came as quite a shock… overwhelming fears of suffocation, all kinds of irritation, and an intense desire for breathing space, freedom, and a return to single-hood. How disturbing, that the distance between us was not yielding to a geographical cure. Living close actually brought up more of the hard stuff, and in a way that was not at all fun. This was not in my plans.

I wrote a hard rock song to vent.

Love Is Intrusive

I know you love me, I know you care
But can't you love me, from over there?
You say you just want to be close to me
But that just screws up all my privacy
You say relax, Scott, and just receive
But how can I do that if I can't breathe?

Love is intrusive, it's cramping my style
You are a landline, and I'm a mobile
You've got my number, but hold the phone
Love is intrusive, it won't leave me alone!

I saw a shrink for some consoling
She said my mom was too controlling
And now you're flushing out these issues
I hit some pillows and used some tissues
It's so outrageous, and so ironic
That my beloved, is my colonic
I love you truly, I love you tons
But when you're near me, I get the runs
I want to run, and do some laps
To run away from, feeling so trapped
It was so easy, back when we dated
But now I feel too…domesticated!

Love is intrusive, it doesn't make sense
Love is cathartic, it's so darn intense
Love is invasive, it's right in your face
Love is intrusive, I need me some space!

2004 @ ScottSongs

For the record, Venus was not actually invading my space. She did not sound or act like anyone, either parent or lover, from my past. And yet my past pain was surfacing, screaming for some kind of resolution. I had uprooted and replanted my entire life to be closer, sweeter, and more intimate with my sweetheart, not to recoil and run the other way. I had thought I was done dealing with major childhood issues. The way they just showed up and barged in unannounced was inconvenient, unwelcome, and downright rude!

Moving through these extreme feelings so I could show up for this relationship was now my biggest priority. The universe demonstrated its support by dramatically slowing down my troubadour travels. Suddenly, all at the same time, a number of regular gigs stopped scheduling me. It seemed like a huge conspiracy to get me to stay put and work on my issues. But just how was I supposed to do that? For a while I didn't have a clue.

One date night out Venus asked me to ride a huge roller coaster with her. I agreed, mostly out of wanting to promote a fearless (macho) image. *Hey, no problem. I'm a man's man.* It was only after sitting down in the front car and looking way up that I remembered the fear of heights that had gripped me since childhood. It was roller coasters like this that in my distant past severely challenged my biological ability to retain ownership of the contents of my stomach. (I believe the technical term is *throw-up ride.*) Just as I was entertaining options for a graceful exit, the safety bar locked into place. I felt locked in, but not at all safe. We started going up at a snail's pace, agonizingly slowly. Since I was forgetting to avail myself of the simple pleasures of breathing, the pace was torture. Panic gripped me...belly knotted in protest, knees shaking, dizzy with fear. What had I gotten myself into? Damn my codependency and macho tendencies!

Suddenly the ride went *down.* Sharply. I wondered why anyone would pay money for an experience like this. Yet all around me there were children totally loving it. While I gripped the safety bar as if my life depended on it, those crazy kids were screaming and waving their hands high in the air. And Venus was smiling and laughing right next to me. What was I missing? What did they all know that I didn't?

Just when I was about to throw up, pass out, or both, I remembered to call spiritual 911 and ask for immediate ride-side assistance. My higher self responded right away with a roller coaster rescue remedy:

"EXPRESS YOURSELF!! MOVE THE ENERGY! SCREAM, SCOTT, SCREAM!!!"

I did, bloody murder! I threw a primal tantrum and held nothing back. Instantly everything changed. A tingling, thrilling excitement coursed throughout my body, and laughter bubbled up and out. My need to be on the ground (and in control) dissolved into exhilaration and trust. It was so much fun I wanted to ride again.

Could what I learned on the roller coaster somehow be applied to the dizzying ups and downs of the relationship? I was beginning to suspect it could. After Alana, I had had it with emotional roller coasters and being swept off my feet. I stayed on the ground, and didn't let women close enough to my heart to risk being taken for a ride.

When Venus and I were long distance dating, I was able to stay conscious. But when I moved close, unconscious patterns took over, and I took on the habit of shrinking and playing it small around her, just like I had with my mother, giving up my voice and power by playing a role of *Yes, Dear.* That's what was triggering the intense feelings and desires for space. When I was not using my voice, hers seemed way too loud. When I did not have the nerve to say no, to say *ouch,* to ask for what I wanted, and to simply maneuver freely around Venus, she got on *my* nerves. Reversing this tendency was my work, and it was not easy. I had a lot of resistance to taking responsibility for my part in the dance. It was so much easier to get mad at her for seeming to step on my toes.

Of course, my inner critic was ecstatic that Venus was in my life: it gave me somebody new and special to blame. I excelled at assigning her the role of the cause of my pain. Yet my prosecuting attorney's case against her could hardly hold up in the light of her consistent kindness and fairness. Yes, she did get impatient and pushy with me on occasion, but usually she owned her stuff and apologized before the sun would set. And she actually welcomed my authenticity when I had the courage to go there. She was clearly a keeper. I was the one I wasn't so sure about. And for this relationship to last, I was going to need some kind of emotional makeover, perhaps even divine intervention.

I was guarded and distant more often than not, certainly more often than either one of us was enjoying. At times I would protect my freedom like a wounded animal cornered and fighting for its turf. I swung like a pendulum from the extremes of giving to her without including my feelings in the mix (*Yes, Dear*) to a place of rigid retreat, closed heart, and emotional shut down.

Sometimes Venus took my process in stride, and other times she felt frustrated and stretched to her edge. She was learning about relaxing, trusting, and surrendering to divine timing versus clinging to her own. She was working on growing beyond some old myths and fairy tales, such as having a soulmate and a baby would save and complete her. While she wasn't tossing overboard any of her dreams of having a happy family, she was learning to hold them more lightly and trust that the river was taking her where she needed to go instead of paddling madly upstream, trying to force and push things (like me!) to make them happen. She was also practicing holding herself true, when I wavered and wobbled, to a steady sense of her own worthiness. In short, Venus was also growing through the challenges. As hard as it was to swallow sometimes, the relationship was just the right medicine for both of us.

Four times during our first four years we seriously discussed parting ways. While in those tumultuous periods both of us worked hard to find a middle ground between, on the one hand, too much accommodating and compromising, and, on the other, digging in our heels and clinging to a position as if our very survival was at stake. Each time one or both of us would have some kind of shift, enough to keep the relationship alive and moving forward.

The last time we considered breaking up, it was the child conversation coming to a head once again. My head was camped out at, "I'm not ready and you can't make me!", especially when it sounded like she was saying, "Choose now or I'm leaving." The big question I was wrestling with was: Is my resistance to having a child springing from my deep-down-core-level non-negotiable truth, or is it mostly about fears I could eventually work through? I was trying to find my clarity in the thick of some pretty dense fog.

I knew I loved being around children. I also knew I was about to lose Venus if I did not come up with an authentic yes. That felt huge. Meditation, prayer, counseling, and a few trusted friends all helped me dig deeper, and I came up with something I felt I could live with and possibly grow into. "Venus, how about we begin working on conceiving a child in two years, and starting right now we focus on creating financial stability and abundance so we have that in place before a baby arrives." She agreed, and we kissed and shook on it.

Sometimes it felt more like a settlement arrived at in the courtroom of my mind, and not a commitment discovered in the depths of my heart. Was I shape shifting myself too much so as to not lose love? I still wasn't sure if it had been my very deepest and most authentic self talking, or if my codependency had kicked in and was striking a deal, buying more time…in other words, doing whatever it took to not have to live without Venus.

On my own, I had never owned a pet, or even a plant that needed water more than once a week. I did my troubadour traveling solo, with meditation cushion and low maintenance houseplants waiting for me at home. Having a baby, I knew, would rock my cozy world more than anything else. A child would change forever, could even destroy, the *me*-centered life that had for so long defined, well, *me*. It all seemed so confining, suffocating, terrifying. And it would certainly mean that I was sticking with Venus. I would not consider it an option to have a child with her and then leave because it wasn't easy or fun.

I felt some relief with the idea that I could put the whole thing off for at least two years. Maybe by then I'd be willing and ready.

Hopefully, I'd even be excited about it. After all, from early on in our relationship, Venus could easily see me becoming a natural and awesome dad. She held the vision of us becoming a loving family, and doing it with lots of originality, creativity, and joy. Perhaps she was on to something. Maybe she was the leader in this aspect of the relationship, and maybe it was my lesson to trust her lead, while I stumbled ahead, right on through my doubts and fears.

When Venus let me know that we were pregnant, we both experienced a combination of warm, tingling excitement and chilling anxiety, with Venus leaning more towards the thrill and me towards the chill. We lay down and snuggled in close, prayed together, and listened for guidance. What I heard was, "Life more abundant, incredibly more abundant, is coming in. Let it."

Aysia (pronounced like the continent) somehow snuck right past the gates of birth control, as secure as we thought they were, only a few months after my insecure yes. She was born in the corner of our living room in a rented birthing tub, almost exactly twelve months from when Venus and I had come to our wobbly agreement. It does not take advanced math skill to surmise the surprise she was.

I had no choice but to re-arrange the marbles in my head…to surrender my tidy images of perfection, *my* timing…the notion that I'm somehow in control of *my* life. That illusion was obliterated by Aysia's arrival. My ego's house, the walls and ceilings I had thought defined me and kept me safe, were flattened by hurricane force winds. Divine intervention had arrived, and it blew off the roof as it blew open my heart.

It was not instant and it was not smooth, the transformation of Scott B.C. (Before Child) to a willing, grateful, and even beaming father. There were plenty of grumbles, protests, and even a couple of tantrums along the way as I freaked out about our finances and grieved the loss of my old life. Two things helped me shift. The first was Venus being so vulnerable and needing me to be there for her. That opened my heart and inspired me to show up like I never had before. The second was the emerging personality of Aysia Grace. Her smiles, her laughter, her total dependence on us, all gradually awakened a dormant Daddy, just as nature designed it.

Aysia is a year and a half as I write this, and is thriving and flourishing. Venus and I are as well. Our greatest asset is having a knack for taking turns going crazy. One person staying sane while the other loses it goes a long way in moving through things and not getting stuck in them. Once in a while we both freak out and butt heads, yet most of the time, most days, the shared desire and commitment to be there for Aysia and to be a happy family has helped us to get off of our ego butts quickly and return to living harmoniously.

Nothing is perfect. We face and grow through new challenges all the time. But there is such sweetness and love in the air between us now. We start our day by putting on a song and dancing together as a family. As we dance, sing, and play with our daughter, Venus and I get to revisit, even reclaim, the innocence and preciousness of childhood.

Reading to Aysia is heavenly, the loveliest thing I've ever experienced. She runs to my lap with her current favorite (today it's

Go, Dog, Go!), plops herself down, and instantly my pressing adult priorities become not so pressing. What else is more important?

Last month Aysia started singing. Her latest hits are *Twinkle Twinkle Little Star, The Wheels On The Bus, and The Itsy Bitsy Spider*. Though far from getting the lyrics down perfectly, she belts them out with joy, purity, and passion. She does not wait till she has the words down before jumping in. She knows the secret to learning language, songs, and perhaps the secret to happiness...let your voice ring out, take risks, make a million mistakes, keep learning and growing, have loads of fun, and be a beginner forever.

And for me, learning to love and be loved continues to have its ups and downs, but with Venus and Aysia along to enjoy the ride, I'm no longer sitting out and avoiding the roller coaster. In fact, I'm beginning to put my hands up in the air and say, "Whee"!

Freedom Child

Freedom child, your music can be trusted
Freedom child, there's a symphony at play
Freedom child, the adult just got busted
And a child shall lead the way

When you've been hiding behind the rules
I will throw you in the pool
Inviting you to be a fool
Cause life's a playground, not a school

Hello, I am your long lost part
The freedom child in your heart of hearts
Childlike, but not childish
Playful, but not powerless
Responsible to freedom's call
Driving all the slave drivers up the wall!

When you're possessed by your perfectionist
I will be your exorcist
I can drive the demons out
Save your smile from your pout

I'll break all of your eggshells one by one
Expand your straight and narrow
With a little thing called fun

The freedom child can cut you loose
When your head is hanging in a noose
Cause life is too precious, life is too short
To be a full time worrywart!

When you've been dried up from all the rules
I will throw you in the pool
Inviting you to be a fool
Cause life's a playground, not a school

I'll break all of your eggshells one by one
Expand your straight and narrow
With a little thing called fun

Childlike, but not childish
Playful, but not powerless
Flying free and limitless
Freedom Child!

2004 © *ScottSongs*

Venus, Aysia and Scott 2010

About Scott

Are you serious? This entire book has been about Scott! But for those of you who want the standard back of the book bio thing...

Scott Grace (*formerly Scott Kalechstein*), lives in Marin, California with his lovely partner Venus, and their darling daughter Aysia. He is a writer/coach/comedian/speaker, as well as a singer/songwriter/recording artist/minister and workshop leader. He shares his uplifting music and messages at conferences, corporations, workshops, living rooms, schools, parties, churches, synagogues, weddings, private gatherings-wherever people are open to a lighthearted, humorous and entertaining approach to personal growth and entertainment. Scott's work promotes a sense of joy, safety, community, and playful celebration. His music sometimes evokes laughter, at other times tears, and people are often found singing and clapping and sometimes dancing along while he performs.

A pioneer in the field of intuitive song, Scott is known for his unique ability to spontaneously create songs for individuals or groups, about any topic presented. His "Song Portraits" are a unique display of creativity, and always leave people deeply touched, delighted and amazed by such an in-the-moment creation.

Born and raised in Brooklyn, Scott started studying classical music at age seven with the violin, practicing daily and excelling to the top of his class. Spontaneity was always bursting out of him, sometimes getting him into mischief and trouble. In the orchestras he played in, often he would memorize a piece, put away the sheets of music, and play by heart, both dazzling and annoying the conductor as he embellished the classics with his own creative *improvements*. At age fourteen he started taking guitar lessons. Succumbing to the pull of adolescence, he rebelled against classical violin in favor of jazz and rock n roll guitar. Roll over, Beethoven!

At the advent of college came much spiritual searching, which led him to *A Course in Miracles*, psychotherapy, the 12 Steps, a plethora of self-improvement workshops, rebirthing, meditation, and other activities of self-discovery. During that time he began to write and sing songs about personal and planetary transformation. With the help of singing lessons and the encouragement of friends, Scott set out on a road less traveled to become a professional recording artist and motivational entertainer.

He lived in New York City, selling laundry bags illegally on the sidewalks of the city to pay the bills. Gradually, his concerts and workshops increased in attendance and popularity until 1990, when he sold his last laundry bag and at last became a (universal) law-abiding citizen. Scott moved to California, and embarked full time into his life's work/play.

Currently with nine compact discs being distributed internationally, Scott travels as a transformational troubadour, giving inspirational talks sweetened with music and presenting inspirational comedy concerts salted and peppered with his story telling. Groups large and small seek him out to provide ice breaking, community building, celebration, humor and heart to their events. He has performed at the talks and workshops of popular authors and seminar leaders such as Deepak Chopra, Marianne Williamson, Alan Cohen, Byron Katie, Jack Canfield, Dr. John Gray, Dr. Bernie Siegel, and Barbara DeAngelis. Scott also conducts a variety of workshops of his own.

When he leads these workshops he is quick to make himself vulnerable, sharing his realness...the fumblings, bumblings, learnings and triumphs of his own life. Of course, in all his talks and workshops he uses original songs to take the messages from an intellectual understanding to a heartfelt emotional level. And that is what Scott's music, his message and his life are about, living from the heart.

Bio Rhythms

(A Synopsis in Song)

I was born at a young age in 1963
Survived the streets of Brooklyn and my noisy family
My parents thought God was a scam, religion was for saps
For me that meant no Hebrew School
So I thanked God for that!

No Chanukah, no Christmas trees, no holy holidays
When we gathered for a meal for grace we said "Oy Vey!"
I was schooled in logic, learned hard science and new math
I had some signs of ADD and couldn't sit still in class

I took two years of college and then called it graduation
You could say I left to get a higher education
I became a spiritual seeker, meditation, LSD
I did rebirthing, got real high and met with God drug free!

My parents were beside themselves "Oh, where did we go wrong?
Our son has got religion...well, at least he's not reborn!"
I didn't join a church, or pass pamphlets door to door
I learned to mind my ego so it wouldn't mind the store

I took the latest workshops and expensive weekend trainings
I paid for Tony Robbins to say "Scott, just quit complaining!"

I did my daily practices and found some peace and power
I started writing happy songs and singing in the shower

Some friends who overheard me asked "Why don't you make a tape?
Your music will help many folks rejoice and celebrate"
And so I went from shower to the studio and stage
I freed up the performer who'd been locked inside a cage

My music brought me so much joy and even brought me money
I left the day job, moved out west to where it's much more sunny
I made CD's, the word caught on till I was quite sought after
There's nothing like a message that is sent in song and laughter

At home I learned my lessons just like everybody else
I learned to love another I first gotta love myself
I grew through my relationships, the land of Mars and Venus
I learned to listen to my heart not just my head and penis

So now I journey with a mate, we raise a child together
We're learning we can choose to love in every kind of weather
Sometimes when our fears collide, we both get out of joint
We point the finger at each other and truly miss the point

Yet in the midst of challenges we're learning to stay friends
To welcome different points of view and not judge or defend
A fighting Brooklyn boy can grow to be a gentle man
When he gives up being right and seeks to understand

And that's what I have learned so far out in the Sunshine State
It's best to battle with my ego instead of with my mate
Yes, that's what I have learned in all these years I've told you of
I'd rather lose an argument and win at choosing love
I'd rather drop the arguments and join with you in love

2010 @ *ScottSongs*

Scott's Services & Music

Comic Keynotes

Scott loves serving as a keynote speaker for corporate, holistic health, educational, and service groups, as well as personal growth and church conferences and retreats. Scott brings a blend of warmth, wisdom, and outrageous humor to his presentations. He consistently leaves audiences feeling uplifted, renewed, and enthused. Scott spices up his talks with his original songs, many of them created in the moment in answer to audience questions and requests.

Scott can offer a keynote lecture or interactive seminar, as you wish, and tailor his presentation to your group's unique goals and needs.

Some Program Themes include:

- Loving Relationships Don't Happen to the Lucky, They Happen to the Skilled

- Levity as a Cure for Gravity, Laughter as a Remedy for Fear

- Incurable Optimism, Unreasonable Happiness

- Meditation: The Benefits of a Witness Protection Program

- Emotional Intelligence for Dummies

- Firing Fear as your Guidance Counselor

Conscious Comedy Concerts

As a stand up comedian, Scott has shared the stage with the likes of Robin Williams and Dana Carvey. His musical comedy concerts consistently make people laugh until their cheek muscles are sore. His humor is unique in that he does not lift you up by putting you or others down. There is no hard edge. Instead, the laughs come from both Scott's masterful musical improvisations and his ability to channel the Big Joke through Celestial Cosmic Comedy. With venues as intimate as a house concert and as large as Carnegie Hall, which he has sold out many times in his mind, Scott's concerts are a one of a kind enlightening up experience!

Next Step Coaching

Whether desiring to create a loving relationship or a prosperous career doing what you love, all success depends upon getting clear what your next small step is and then taking it. And then the next step. And the next. That's where coaching can help, both by assisting you in discovering your next step, and calling you to action.

With heart-centered wisdom, gentleness, and a powerful laser beam of intuitive insight, Scott adores helping individuals and couples find their passion, go for their dreams, and create happy, harmonious relationships. Scott's specialties are conscious dating and mating, inner critic and inner child healing, quantum creativity, Nonviolent Communication, grief-work, emotional healing, and building unconditional self-love and self-esteem. He has been coaching people since 1995.

> *"Scott helped me through a difficult communication challenge at work with my boss. The specific tools he taught me were perfect for resolving the situation and I have continued to use them more and more successfully in other situations. Scott has an enormous capacity to create emotional safety and trust very quickly and gracefully. He also has a masterful handle on using and teaching Nonviolent Communication skills. I would recommend him to anyone who needs help getting through a difficulty or is ready to take their next step in achieving their goals."*

> ~ Susan S, Bookkeeper, Novato, CA

Scott's Workshops

The Conscious Relationship Workout is a fun and vigorous workout in the mental and emotional gym to help you get in better shape for relationship as a path of growth, healing, and awakening. The workout is designed to support anyone wanting a relationship, enjoying a relationship, facing challenges in a relationship, or recuperating from a relationship! It is filled with processes, tools, songs, and heart-centered wisdom for the voyage that relationship entails. *Warning: Contents under pressure. The workout may not be suitable for those attached to looking for love in all the wrong places, namely outside of yourself, and might cause considerable pressure to outgrow unconscious relationship habits and beliefs modeled after fairy tales and country and western songs.*

The Greatest Love of All is a workshop on learning to love, honor and marry yourself for life. Scott shares both the art and the science of self-love, and gently, powerfully and humorously inspires people to abandon the self-abandonment that has been programmed into everyone in the culture. It is filled with music, laughter, inspiration, and practical tools and practices that you will take home for further expansion and development of the most important love relationship you will ever have: the one with yourself!

Say Yes to Your Dreams is powerful support for finding your passion, living your purpose, and discovering ways to do what you love and get paid lucratively for it. Scott shares inspiration from his own journey, songs, and tools and technologies that help you encourage and empower yourself to take action on behalf of your dreams.

Getting Your YAH YAH'S Out is about connecting with your true YAH YAH'S, the delicious and divine antics of your unbridled aliveness, your untamed creative self-expression. This is a safe and silly space for you to set free the innocent playfulness that your inner critic might be censoring. In fact, any and all censorship is censored at the playshop! The world needs your YAH YAH's out, not in. Your overly responsible and rigid adult mask that you may have been mistaking for your true self will lighten up considerably, and transform from being in critical condition to easily achieving spontaneous emissions.

Teach Me How To Love contains practices, exercises, humor, wisdom, and songs that support the healing, opening, and awakening of the heart so that we can ever more deeply let ourselves love and be loved.

The Song Portrait Circle is an opportunity for a small group of people to gather to share the experience of receiving Song Portraits, intuited personal healing songs that powerfully support each individual's unique journey through life.

"Scott accomplished more in a three hour workshop than most therapists achieve in three years,"

~ Sheila A, Teacher, Huntington Station, NY

Song Portraits By Scott

Done over the phone or in person, for yourself, or for someone special in your life.

Song Portraits are as unique as you are...intuitively composed in the moment and recorded on CD or MP3 for a lifetime of enjoyment and reflection.

Makes an incredible gift to honor and celebrate your loved ones!

Almost always when I am finished giving a Song Portrait, both the person receiving it and I have tears flowing down our cheeks. Many report that listening to their song is like having a cheerleading squad on the sidelines of their life, and that it is particularly helpful in transforming the inner critic that is constantly repeating a negative song. Many play it every morning upon awakening, and/or every night before sleep.

Receive a song to uplift you in your growth process, to support you with relationship issues, grief and loss resolution, career transitions, health concerns, or any sort of life experience.

Do you have a dream that sometimes seems bigger than you? Keep your vision fueled with a song that will inspire and empower you in the direction of your dreams.

Affirm accomplishments. Integrate life's highlights more deeply. Celebrate the special moments on the journey of life: graduations, weddings, anniversaries, babies, career moves, etc. Honor your uniqueness & contribution to the world. Celebrate yourself or someone you love in song.

"Scott, the song portrait you sang for Barb and I stands out as one of the most memorable and healing experiences of my life."

~ Larry A, Arden, North Carolina

CD Discography

(In Order of Popularity)

Levitational Pull 1998
Songs for Enlightening Up!

Eighteen playful, joyous, lighthearted and often hysterically humorous personal growth related songs reminding you to lighten up and let in the light. Swami Beyondananda finds it *"...witty, wise, funny and entertainin...the perfect antidote for seriousness. Levitational Pull will help you defy gravity!"*

Midwives of the Light 1995
Songs for Personal & Planetary Rebirth

This music is offered as support for transitional times in our lives...to help us accept, embrace, and even celebrate change. It's for when our sense of self, or our current planet of residence may be going through a cleanse cycle in the Divine Washing Machine. Let these songs be anthems of trust, bathing you in comfort and reminding you of your strength. Heartsong Review reports: *"Scott's music gets better and better. I loved his last album, The Eyes of God, but he has surpassed the high standards he set then to give us a perfect collection of songs that range from devotional to celebratory, always engaging and heart-stirring."*

The Eyes of God 1994
Mantras and Sing-a-longs for the Soul

These devotional and deeply heart-centered songs will be your precious companions and mantras as you open to Love's Presence in your life. Featuring an angelic choir and the vocal blessings of recording artists Donna Cary and Charley Thweatt, musically supported by the exquisite sounds of classical guitar, fretless bass, soprano saxophone and much, much, more. Awareness Magazine calls it *"a spiritual massage, caressing and nurturing the heart."* Great for meditation, prayer, making love, or whenever you need a reminder of the Sacred.

Something New 2004
Romantic, Uplifting, Lighthearted Jazz Tunes

From The Light Connection Magazine: *"The album is truly a masterful collaboration, with Scott's vocals moving with the band from one style to another (jazz, pop, samba and swing) with the ease of a cat jumping up on a fence. At times smooth and liquid, then full and spicy, he rocks us and cajoles us and makes us want to push 'Play' again and again when it's done."*

Love Songs 1999
For the Heart's Awakening

Twelve songs written, arranged & performed with masterful musicianship and production to provide opening, enjoyment, healing and assistance on the journey toward greater heart connection and intimacy, both with a partner and with Life. It includes empowered romantic love songs (completely free of co-dependent lyrics!) and spiritual and planetary love songs as well. Repeated listening will soften your heart, smoothing out the rough edges of your soul.

Let There Be Light 1993
Songs of Joy, Hope and Healing

This double recording features 28 of Scott's greatest hits from the years 1988 to 1993. Over two hours of music is packed into this selection. CD #1 consists of mellow, meditative, and devotional songs. CD#2 is upbeat, uplifting, moving, and motivational. These songs are not repeated on any other CD's.

Putting the Pieces Together 1992
For The Children in your Life and the Child in your Heart

Heartsong Review says: *"Fantastic! Filled with fun, energetic music for kids of all ages. The lyrics are funny with great stories that convey positive messages with first-rate music from a well-rounded band. Fabulous for ages 5-100!"*

Maps for the New World 2002
Songs that Point the Way

This recording contains fifteen songs, 68 minutes of music ranging from humorous and playful to soulful and deeply healing planetary anthems. *"The entire CD vibrates with uplifting energy, inspiration and mirth. The variety leaves something for every mood, and I can't help but smile as I listen to it."*

-A Happy Customer

To inquire about any of the services above, to order more copies of this book, to sample, purchase, or download any of Scott's music CD's, or to sign up to stay connected and be on his email list:

visit www.scottsongs.com
email info@scottsongs.com
or call 1-877-591-8863.